INSANELY GIFTED

TURN YOUR DEMONS INTO CREATIVE ROCKET FUEL

JAMIE CATTO

CANONGATE

Edinburgh · London

Published in Great Britain in 2016 by Canongate Books Ltd,
14 High Street, Edinburgh EH1 1TE

www.canongate.tv

2

British Library Cataloguing-in-Publication Data
A catalogue record for this book is available on
request from the British Library

ISBN 978 1 78211 803 9

Typeset in Garamond 3 by Palimpsest Book Production Ltd,
Falkirk, Stirlingshire

Printed and bound in Great Britain by Clays Ltd, St Ives plc.

INSANELY GIFTED

Jamie Catto runs personal development workshops worldwide. His teaching builds on his own experience of overcoming creative hurdles, and provides techniques that invite everyone to fulfil their potential. He was also a founding member of dance mega-group Faithless and acclaimed global music and philosophy project 1 Giant Leap.

Contents

Introduction

There was a time during my late teenage years when, night after night, with no discernible trigger, my body would descend into a state of primal terror. I found myself more and more terrified as the day drew on, knowing that as the light began to fade I would be back there in hell again, isolated, dying inside.

As soon as it got dark, I would feel a tingling around my perineum and then extreme nausea would take over, coupled with a rising, galloping thudding of the heart as adrenaline flooded my system. Over the next hours I would be back and forth to the toilet, first vomiting whatever was in my stomach and later retching bile and air when my stomach had nothing left to offer. I had no way to make this stop and it would only cease when I finally fell into exhausted unconsciousness, drenched in the stinking, clammy sweat of fear.

Back in the 1980s they didn't really have the term 'panic attacks', and so no one knew what was going on when out of the blue I would start shaking and vomiting and disappear into a foetus-like state. It was so intense that after a few months of experiencing this every single night I felt the only option open to me was to kill myself. At the time, my mum had got involved in a self-development course called Turning Point, run by a genius Australian facilitator called Graham Browne. She had been trying to get me to attend the course with evangelic verve yet I found the whole thing completely creepy. The more she tried to get me to do it, the more I resisted and judged her for her cliquey, new-age language, but when I came to her and said, 'Mum, I'm not being dramatic, but I think I might need to kill myself. I can't handle much more of this, and if it is this or nothing, night after night, I think I choose nothing,' she looked at me coolly, didn't try to talk me out of it and said, 'Look, just try going on this weekend, and if it hasn't shifted it by Monday, then kill yourself. Deal?' Who could argue with that?

The course *was* powerful, and even though it wasn't a one-stop healing for my condition it definitely changed something about my responsibility and willingness to feel all my feelings and reframe what might be happening in me. It taught me to stop and look at what was going on, to notice and observe myself rather than be totally taken over by the experience.

It was the beginning of a great treasure hunt, the first step on a journey that has brought me years of making films and music and running workshops, and now even coaching people with panic attacks. This road of exploration led me to many different practices, ideas and breathing techniques through the many cultures I visited and studied, all thanks to trying to survive being so sensitive in this world.

In 1999 this journey took me around the world with a project called 1 Giant Leap. The first trip was a journey of collaboration with singers and musicians from fifty countries, and along the way we also interviewed writers, chiefs, gurus, criminals and street kids. It was fascinating to me that the more diversity we encountered, the more unity was expressed. And the thing I realised so many of us human beings shared was this collective insanity, an unspoken pact where we all waste a huge amount of our daily energy maintaining an appearance of confidence and 'being fine'-ness in public – especially at work, where being a 'winner' and 'on top of things' is paramount. I witnessed the way we will go to such extreme lengths to avoid our pain and our shadows, which for me resulted in those teenage panic attacks. I realised how many of us hide our true faces behind masks of appropriateness and how much shame and embarrassment we feel for the uniquely beautiful, eccentric and wounded individuals we are.

And here is the big clue about our suffering. If it weren't for the heinous panic attacks I suffered in my late teens and the suicidal state I got myself into, I would never have sought out information and techniques to pull myself out of the misery. The survival tools I have learned have taught me to be a skilful and empathic helper for those who are experiencing similar things. I notice that the hardest times of my life have acted as a kind of superhero training, sculpting me and giving me gifts which are useful for others in need. It is almost as if, in our suffering, we are sent down into the darkest mines alone, but when we return to the surface we notice that we have in our hand a jewel that is of use to the next person down the line struggling as we have been.

In order to survive, I discovered that I had to be willing to feel my pain if I was ever going to release it, I had to be willing to stop hiding so much of myself that I judged as unattractive or inappropriate. If I was ever going to feel connected to the world around me I had to be willing to feel vulnerable, to go to the edge, come what may, and stop worrying so much about what might happen when I got there.

When they asked Michelangelo about his epic *David* sculpture, he said that as soon as they brought him the huge slab of rock he could already see the figure of David standing there within it. His job was just to chip away the excess marble, and that's what we're doing here with our innate genius. I want to invite you to slowly come out of hiding in all your raw glory and begin to dissolve that massive knot of emotional, painful gunk inside. I want you to tear up the complicit agreement that tells us all to say we're fine when anyone asks. We so rarely feel safe enough to say what is really going on. So I have entered the rock-dissolving business, and the many exercises throughout this book are designed to help you dissolve your own rocks and make a Masterpiece of yourself.

It has dawned on me that we are all functioning, relating and creating from such an insanely limited version of our true potential that our brief seventy or so years of human experience are as good as wasted while we scurry around worrying and controlling and battling our way through our limited, self-cherishing lives. I want every aspect of my life and yours to be a Masterpiece, I want my work to be a Masterpiece, I want my parenting to be a Masterpiece, I want my sex life and all my relationships to be Masterpieces. I want us to explore the edges, gently, to laugh at our foolishness, gently, and see ourselves for everything that we are.

I want to live in a world where we stop settling for operating at this drastically reduced capacity and un-edit ourselves back to the juicy, unapologetic, uniquely gifted humans we really are. This is what I feel passionate about, what I am an activist for, because if you're going to rebel against anything, best to start with our own considerable bondage. We are enslaved by our approval addictions, our fear of what people might think, our competitiveness, our shame of who we really are, and all this is death to intimacy and death to our Masterpieces. If you want to engage fully with your passion and innate genius, this is where to start . . .

Bob Geldof maintains that he never felt saintly about his work to end poverty in Africa; it just really annoyed him that such a solvable situation was going on unsorted. This is how I feel about the way we're all going through our lives as these violently edited-down potential versions of ourselves. It irritates me in the worst way to see most of us humans living so dishonestly with ourselves and others and, in our quest for safety and comfort, missing out. It isn't complicated, but just because something is simple doesn't mean it is easy. When we dare to be visible, when we stop hiding, when we commit to staying present with our feelings instead of numbing them and escaping them, suddenly our lives turn from black and white into colour.

I'm on a mission, through my films and music, through my workshops, and now this book, to create an army of 'walking permission slips', a legion of like-minded souls who, just by being themselves, present, authentic, often vulnerable, become catalysts for everyone who comes into contact with them. When we meet people like this, who are comfortable to be seen and heard just as they are without hiding behind roles or being an 'appropriate' version of themselves, we ourselves become more relaxed and more authentic. Our freedom to be seen in our mess, in our eccentricity, in our fallibility, creates a permission in everyone we meet to lighten up around all the sides of ourselves that we believe aren't welcome, and when that happens, intimacy and creativity levels shoot through the roof.

THE MANIFESTO

- We want to put our own full, unedited, unabbreviated selves into the work.
- We want to create a movement of introspection and self-enquiry where the viewer becomes the subject of the piece. It's about you.
- We want to dare to show ourselves in all our raw glory, really express what's going on in the chaos and the shadows, then give ourselves the chance to connect to something real in our audience. Because when I talk about me, you'll hear about you.
- We need to collectively admit that we're not fine, we're not confident and balanced and good.
- We turn up to work every day pretending we're not neurotic and obsessed and insatiable and full of doubt, and we waste so much energy keeping up this mutual pretence for each other because we think if people saw the truth, if people really knew what was going on in our heads, all the crazy truth of our dark appetites and self-loathing, then we'd be rejected. But in fact, the opposite is true. It is when we dare to reveal the truth that we unwittingly give everyone else permission to do the same.
- We need to stop holding our breath for a moment and actually come into the room. Be here, present, vulnerable and authentic.
- If we can all collectively acknowledge our insanity, the amount of energy we'll inherit that has been wasted on the mask will be enough to creatively solve any global crisis. We are on a mission to make self-reflection hip for just a moment, just long enough to save us.

CHAPTER 1

How We All Became Approval Addicts

No man, for any considerable period, can wear one face to himself and another to the multitude, without finally getting bewildered as to which may be the true.

Nathaniel Hawthorne, *The Scarlet Letter*

Imagine for a moment if everyone could hear the running commentary in your head – your colleagues, your friends, your lover. What's really going on beneath the surface you present to the world? Do you find yourself constantly placating and saying what you think others wish to hear? Do you ever get the feeling you are a fraud and one day you are going to get found out?

When we're born into this world we are totally helpless. Unlike horses and other creatures who are almost immediately up on their feet the moment they are born, because of our lovely, large human brain, a baby's head would be too big to make it through its mother's birth canal if it was fully gestated, so the last chapter of 'pregnancy' has to happen outside the womb. Consequently the human baby, when it first emerges, is in need of total care and education from day one: how to eat, how to walk, how to hold and manipulate objects, how to communicate, all the basic functions of a person. These skills need to be taught to the new child by parents and carers, and the most common and seemingly efficient way we've found to teach our children is to give them loads of gushing approval and love when they 'get it right' or obey us, and when they don't, give them less, or none. Children's main source of safety and survival is the love from their parents and carers, so the discomfort or even trauma for that source of nourishment to be turned on and off is very impactful. Each of us, when we were being brought up and 'taught how to be a person' had the experience of this on/off approval and love. When we give something great but then withhold it, and then give something great but then withhold it, what that creates in the human is an *addiction*. We have all been unwittingly turned into little approval addicts throughout our childhoods, with a deeply ingrained fear of criticism or failure because we equate that with 'less love' or even 'rejection'.

This value system is backed up all the way through school, too. If you're first in the class, or win the race, you get endless love and praise and validation, and if you're bottom of the class or last in the race you're less appreciated and even, in some cases, shamed. Most kids get the message that to 'do it right' and be 'good and appropriate' is essential if you are to be loved and welcomed and not rejected or emotionally exiled. The addiction to being high up the league table of approval is so compelling that even though brothers and sisters love each other, are each other's main playmate, the moment that one of them does something against the rules, the other sibling will likely run straight to Mummy and Daddy to report the transgression, all for the prize of being higher in the approval rating.

We are so addicted to approval that we even needed to invent Facebook. 'Ahhh, I got seventeen likes under my Rumi quote.' Yum yum yum.

The real problems begin when we don't just get approval withheld, but we get some unexpected, angry negative feedback from our parents and carers. 'Stop that! That's disgusting!' Pow! It hits us in the chest. I remember as a kid once being whacked with a venomously delivered 'When are you going to *grow up*?!', which I felt physically hit me in the body, knocking the emotional wind out of me. We have no idea as children that this adult is just tired or having a bad day, or simply doesn't realise they are being an arsehole. We're too young to have the maturity to screen out their violence and know 'it is their stuff, don't take it on'. We believe it really is our fault they have reacted that way. It is so, so painful that, whatever we were doing when they scolded us, we make a personal note never to be seen doing that again. The possible withdrawal of their love and approval is so frightening and the feeling of the adult's anger is so impactful that we make a little edit in ourselves, hoping never to experience that rejection again. And this goes on and on throughout childhood.

'How could you?' <snip>

'Good girls don't do that!' <suppress>

'Bad boy!' <edit>

Day after day, year after year as we're growing up <snip> <suppress> <edit> <snip> <suppress> <edit> and the violent editing continues with our peers in school, too.

'Oh, you're *so uncool*!'

<Oh, am I? OK, never wear bright colours ever again . . . never dance in public again . . .>

Through this ongoing process of editing out the parts of ourselves that get mirrored to us as 'unwelcome' or 'bad' and only allowing to be seen the parts of us that get love and approval, we arrive as adults presenting a much diminished 'brochure' of ourselves, the shop window of our good bits – an 'appropriate', risk-free version.

Debbie Ford says in *The Dark Side of the Light Chasers* that when we are born we are each a castle with a thousand rooms and each of the rooms has a gift for us. We are completely open, we are curious, adventurous and limitless. Our imaginations and our creativity know no bounds. But as soon as we come into the world our parents tell us, 'Darling, we don't use these rooms over here so much', and so those rooms immediately start getting boarded up. And then throughout our childhoods people walk through our castle and tell us which rooms they like better than others, and more and more rooms fall into disuse, until we arrive as adults believing we are a two-bedroom flat that 'needs some work'.

The big problem is that no Masterpiece ever came out of that place. No touching expressions of art or intimacy were ever born from the sanitised, appropriate versions of ourselves. Whoever heard anyone say 'Have you met Brian? Oh, he's just so . . . appropriate! He turns me *on*!'

The artists and people who touch us deeply are the ones who are not so scared and limited to only express their appropriate qualities. The ones we are moved by are the ones who are brave or eccentric enough to go to the edges of what's normal and safe. We are turned on by those characters, we even deify them as if they are special, as if they are stars. We want to feel those edgier, juicier parts of ourselves but we want to experience them in a safe, controlled way, so the artists and rebels provide that for us. We don't want to experience hanging off a cliff by one arm, sobbing in anguish, but we do like having a vicarious experience of Brad Pitt doing it up on the big screen while we all sit in safe dark rows. There we can cry along safely, or feel terror, or immense, boundless love – all because the artists are willing to really go there. This is why we worship the actors and musicians who deliver these experiences and pay them such incredible amounts of money.

This is the predicament of being human. We want to feel intensity. We want to feel our edges. But only safely within each of our comfort zones. Our problem here is that all our treasure and inspiration is not found in the safe areas furthest inland from our edges. The treasure of our lives, the illuminating and fulfilling experiences, are all discovered by snorkelling around the coastline of the edited version of ourselves, not staying away from them. That doesn't mean we have to trample our boundaries and rush straight out into the deep water proclaiming 'Here are my nipples!', but neither will we ever be available to bring in a Masterpiece of feeling, of intimacy, or creation, by staying as far away from those edges as we can day after day.

BURIED TREASURE

It is not only the 'darker' sides of our nature that we bury and suppress. We imagine that the shadow sides of our nature are the darker qualities like greed and neediness, or our deviant sexual appetites, but if we grew up in a house where something as innocent as our natural flamboyance wasn't supported, then our entertainer nature might very well have been buried in the shadows, too. Most of us were cautioned to quieten down if we were getting excited with everyone's attention, often shamed or muted with irritation by the adults. Well, it doesn't take more than a couple of 'stop showing off in front of your friends' blows to crush that confident entertainer mojo and flavour future flamboyant impulses with some shame or worry about our natural urge to move the crowd.

In another home it might be quietness or shyness that's not acceptable. 'Stand up straight!' 'Speak up for everyone to hear!' 'Don't be a shrinking violet!' And whoever lives in that house is likely to grow up with shame or worry around being too shy.

It is wonderful and often heart-breaking to see some of the attendees of my Transforming Shadows workshops allowing themselves to play with their more 'forbidden' qualities in the safe container of the group. Suddenly a previously meek woman cries with hilarity and relief as she struts around the place being totally bitchy to everyone and those she encounters absolutely love her in it, or a once spiritually, politically correct Buddhist monk gets into people's faces, vocalising extreme judgements about them and letting his unenlightened voices out of the box for ten minutes. Years of lack of permission for these living aspects of themselves, under these safe circumstances, drop away in that game, and there's a sense of wholeness, of coming home, which isn't only a relief to the individual but also to everyone else around them. There's something really uncomfortable, even claustrophobic, about being in the presence of someone else's suppression.

We are each of us uniquely sculpted by our formative years, but the only one who can go in and harvest all that treasure we've buried is us.

The student says to the guru: 'I want liberation.'

The guru replies: 'Who is restraining you?'

The irony is that even though we live in terror of anyone seeing these shameful and unwelcome aspects of ourselves, all the treasure we want for our creativity and our relationships lies buried in the shadows. These parts of ourselves have gifts, they have life, they are full of dimension and intensity, but we've pushed them away for fear of rejection. What if we're missing the real invitation and potential here? As Jung said, if we are willing to explore beyond the 'persona', the mask that we put on during the day, and accept all the defects and ugly bits we find in the shadows, it is then that we get to connect with the source, where our instincts become stronger, our emotions freer and our perceptions wider. My experience is that it is so much more efficient and inspiring to explore ways to play with those buried parts. Some of the greatest and most compelling characters in literature are the villains and the psychos, all born from the darker, less acceptable realms of the writer. It is when the hero goes into the darkest part of the forest that he discovers the gold or the secret of life. It is when the princess is willing to kiss the frog that she finds her prince. If you and I are to be free and play from a full deck then there's nothing we can push away. All that sometimes uncomfortable energy we've been taught not to feel is the fodder for our growth and intimacy. The most touching, melancholy poems and music, the most thrilling sex games and the most genius, evil mischief all arise from the willingness to go beyond this safe and 'appropriate' version of ourselves.

When we allow in more and more of ourselves we become available for intimacy. When I am more visible in who I am, I become a walking permission slip for you to lighten up about your own edges. I invite you to be genuine and relaxed around me instead of manufacturing a 'version' of you which you've groomed to be 'acceptable'. How exhausting! How much of your day is spent wearing masks for people who would only accept you when you wear that mask? Surely these are the very people you don't want to hang out with! Why am I exhausting myself wearing masks for the very people I don't want to hang out with? It has got to be a better idea to gently remove the masks, layer by layer, and see who stays. Those are the people who really love us. Those are the people I want to create with and live with.

By rooting our projects, our art and relationships in visibility we make contact with the authentic nature of whoever comes into contact with us, and that recognition is the intimacy we're all looking for.

CHAPTER 2

Hiding Demons

> Projection of our own shadow makes the whole world a
> replica of our own unknown face.
>
> Carl Jung

How many of us grew up in a family where our rage was supported? Anger is a natural and essential element of the spectrum of human emotion. We all have it, but if, while we were growing up, we were shut down or told off every time we got angry, we soon learned that expressing our rage was unacceptable and would result in a telling off or worse. 'How dare you speak like that to your mother?!' We learn to suppress, not express, our rage, and month after month, year after year, all that non-expression accumulates in us, creating a mini pressure cooker ready to react and explode.

What happens to all those parts of ourselves we attempt to edit away? These essential parts of ourselves are impossible to amputate. The best we can hope to do is suppress them, bury them in the basement somewhere out of sight, but because these aspects of us are alive, it is impossible to eradicate them completely. In fact, ironically, it seems that, like a beach ball pushed down under the water, the deeper we try and bury them the more violently they spring back up. There's a reason they say 'beware the anger of the quiet man'. The more we try to deny and keep a lid on these demons, the more likely they are to suddenly leak into our everyday lives in unexpected, self-sabotaging episodes.

If we are too successful in our suppression, and we bury something so deep that it never gets expressed, then in the dark it continues to grow, but without any outward expression it has to turn inward and become a disease. Life will find its way of expressing, and if we don't participate and allow it to be expressed outwardly in a safe context, as energy can never be cancelled out or destroyed, it finds a way to feed itself in the dark.

REPAIR WITH GOLD

The human body is the most amazing self-mending machine we know of in the universe. We take it for granted of course, but isn't it amazing that when we scratch our skin, it heals itself? If we break a bone, it knits itself back together. Deepak Chopra talks about the human body as being 'an exquisite pharmacy'. While we go about our lives, our body is scanning for viruses and bacteria, it is making its own drugs! Secreting substances from glands and then administering them to us in the perfect quantities day and night while we work, play and sleep.

The body is hard-wired to mend itself, no matter what, but it is not just on the material plane that it is self-mending. It is also hard-wired to mend itself on the emotional and mental planes. Despite all these ways we've edited ourselves down, all the snips and cuts and clever ways we've found to edit away these essential parts of ourselves, the body and Life itself is working round the clock to *un*-edit us, to restore the unapologetic, complete version of ourselves that we began as. Life has no choice but to do this; we are hard-wired to constantly mend ourselves. So no matter how successful we think we are being at manicuring this appropriate person to please the world, Life has other plans. Have you noticed this?

Have you noticed how whatever you push away keeps coming back, knocking at the door? More than that, the deeper you have buried it, the more forcefully it needs to get your attention. The more you deny and disown something, the more Life has to almost break the door down to get to you. There seems to be no escaping yourself. It reminds me of something my folks would say to me when I was not co-operating at bedtime: 'Do you want to go to bed the easy way or the hard way?' As the Zen proverb says, 'Let go or be dragged', because Life will evolve you whether you come kicking and screaming or agree to participate and make it easier on yourself. 'Bedtime' comes for us all, whether we make it easy or hard on ourselves. I have discovered when I become a willing participant in this process my life treats me more gently, but it requires a total reframing of how I've been taught to experience my life.

Most of us have been uploaded with the basic human software, Victim 101, where we view the unexpected and challenging people and situations that cross our paths as problems, as things we have to suffer, as things that are 'happening to us'. It takes a great leap of faith to imagine during these uncomfortable moments that there might be a deeper intelligence at work which is in constant connection to our state of being and doing its best to invite us back to our juicy, unedited selves.

Let's upgrade our internal software from Victim 101 to Warrior 305.

Here's an example: from the usual perspective, the people who irritate us are annoying things we have to put up with, but from the reframing stance of 'Life is trying to show me something' there's a whole new level of data to explore. The person who annoys you might not bug me at all, and you might well be totally immune to the people who drive me crazy. It is almost as if the people who irritate us have been sent over specially by some sort of Central Casting agency to be just the kind of arse-hole who pisses us off. Is it all random or might it be a perfectly designed situation sent or manifested deliberately to give us some sort of a clue?

What I notice is that whatever aspects of myself I have tried to edit out, whatever parts I am disowning or have no permission for in my life, whenever I see other people displaying those characteristics it stirs me up. Whatever I'm not accepting in me I will judge harshly in you. So if I grew up in a house where flamboyance was frowned upon then when I see someone being big and loud I will think to myself, *what an attention whore.* You might be sitting next to me witnessing the same person but because your natural entertainer was never squashed in your home you aren't annoyed by them dancing on the table, you're just enjoying the fun.

Think of the last person who irritated you, and think of the quality they were expressing. Whatever it was, do you have permission to be like that in your life? We all contain the poten-tial to be everything, including greedy and selfish and needy, but these darker parts of ourselves have become so judged, so unwelcome, so rejected, that we have learned to deny our own parts, never let them be seen, and when we see others behaving that way we judge them, as if we ourselves are never like that. But it is nonsense, when you look at it, because we are all a bit greedy sometimes, no? Did you never take more than your share? Or want to? We are all a bit needy, we're all a bit selfish, and because we have no permission for these qualities, seeing others with those qualities feels painful. We feel the shame and the pain of where that unaccepted part lives in us.

So from one point of view these are annoying people, but when we reframe the experience as 'life illuminating us' we see that every annoying person is giving us a living menu of all the aspects of ourselves that we are not accepting. With this framing, the unending list of numbskulls who cross our path is really an educational list of all the ways we are rejecting ourselves, and if you're a willing participant on this journey back to wholeness, it is a list that is useful to have. When we frame them this way, then what used to be annoying people ruining our afternoon becomes a vivid series of illuminations. Instead of being a downer, the experiences give us a chance to be powerful. It depends how you choose to look at it.

Like Me!

Have you noticed how often you make judgements about other people, whether just to yourself or in conversation? For one day, I want you to practise the habit of adding 'like me!' whenever you hear yourself say anything about anyone, good or bad.

For example: 'He's such a great guy, but not always completely

---

honest . . . like me!' 'She's so talented but a bit of an attention-seeker . . . like me!'

It is so liberating.

We can create a lot of false separation and alienation when we describe or pass judgements on others, as if we ourselves are 'not like that'. We separate ourselves from them in our definitions. The truer and more intimate way to live is to shout 'like me!' each time we judge something in another. We all have the potential to act in the darkest and lightest of ways and one major reason we judge is because we want to distance those 'unacceptable' qualities from ourselves. Joyously announcing one's fallibility at every opportunity dissolves this false separation and creates oxygen for everyone to be their perfectly flawed selves without feeling the need to live in hiding.

Once the separation is dissolved, intimacy naturally arises . . .

If you want to see this menu of your disowned parts in action, for one full day, keep track of each and every judgement you place on someone else and every time add the 'like me!' phrase at the end. It will also give you a tidy list of numerous ways you've not, until now, been in acceptance of yourself, and if you're in the mood to be diligent, with a little enquiry, you can dissolve them one by one.

FEEDING MEAT TO THE DEMONS

Life is doing its best to reunite us with all of our disowned parts. They need to find their expression somewhere, hopefully not too destructively in our lives. They are alive, you can't amputate them or 'get rid of' them. So, to avoid them leaking out and sabotaging us or festering away deep inside us and turning into illness, we need to find safe places for these characters to play and breathe and express. The Tibetan Buddhists call this 'feeding meat to the demons'. How can I find ways to play with my deviousness, my violence, my meanness, without actually causing harm to anyone?

There are many realms where this can be explored and played with. Musicians are lucky that they can write a killer punk rock song and express the rage that way. Have you ever met a punk rocker? They're the gentlest souls alive. Why? Because they've channelled all that rage into their art so they're not being yanked this way and that by their anger in their everyday lives. Music – creating and listening to it – is a great tool for enjoying emotions that are less welcome in our everyday lives. Three quarters of all pop music is wallowing in co-dependent love. 'Baby, I need you, I can't live without you, I wanna be the only one to hold you, don't leave, baby, come back . . .' You would never allow yourself (unless totally desperate) to express yourself in such an unbelievably needy way as those lyricists do, but getting swept away in the music of it gives permission to feel those parts of ourselves safely and without shame.

Movies are great for this, too. Of course it is not attractive to be vengeful, but how delicious it is to totally give ourselves to a cinematic story where there's an awful, cruel villain getting his or her comeuppance! We follow a carefully structured path of events, all perfectly timed to deliver us the greatest satisfaction as we witness the baddies getting exactly what they deserve. Those characters are servants for our denied lust for vengeance. Also, literature can perform the same function. I'm reminded of our dear, sweet housekeeper as a child, the nicest, politest woman you could meet, who, once her duties were done, would curl up with a chilling murder thriller.

And, as we've established, it is not only our dark sides that we hide away and disown. Many of us have no permission for our power and heroic natures, too, as if it would be arrogant to stand up and lead. Our inner heroes and heroines have fallen into a bit of disuse, languishing in the shadows as we watch Harrison Ford and Angelina Jolie act them out for us. I love this quote by Marianne Williamson which was included in Nelson Mandela's inaugural speech:

> Our deepest fear is not that we are inadequate. Our deepest fear is that we are powerful beyond measure. It is our light, not our darkness that most frightens us. We ask ourselves, Who am I to be brilliant, gorgeous, talented, fabulous? Actually, who are you not to be? . . . Your playing small does not serve the world. There is nothing enlightened about shrinking so that other people won't feel insecure around you. We are all meant to shine, as children do. We were born to make manifest the glory of God that is within us. It is not just in some of us; it is in everyone. And as we let our own light shine, we unconsciously give other people permission to do the same. As we are liberated from our own fear, our presence automatically liberates others.

THE VOICES IN MY HEAD

It is healthy and necessary for us to follow the heroes and heroines conquering all adversity and winning the day, and it acts as a shadow-expressing exercise. We can vicariously enjoy the victories and bravery that we don't feel ready yet to express in our lives. But art can only give us a watered-down version of our own shadows.

It does not connect with all the parts in us that need to be fed, the parts we've determined are unsafe for public consumption. Similarly, shouting abuse at the referee at the football match every weekend does not quite do the job of fully releasing the amount of rage and injustice many of us carry. It is time to go deeper.

Because we cannot amputate these aspects of ourselves – we cannot fully get rid of the rageful one in us, the controlling one, the bitch, the critic, etc. – and because we work so hard making sure no one else ever discovers they're there, the only place left for them to go is inward. So we end up with a whole legion of characters taking up residence in our heads and giving us a rich and compelling daily inner dialogue that is very hard to ignore. They don't limit themselves just to filling up our heads inescapably but they also, when triggered, make use of all our body's alarm chemicals, churning our bellies and adrenalising our bloodstreams with galloping hearts.

All the time I'm head tripping about something, turning some situation over and over in my mind, be it obsessing with the future or the past, I am missing my life, and I can never get that wasted time back. I'd better have a very good reason to spend time meticulously deconstructing the past because every minute I spend doing it I'm missing the Now where another, more immediate experience is happening and available – and will never be repeated. Is what happened before so precious that it deserves double time? Being a puppet on a string yanked left and right by whatever worry or regret my mind chooses to offer up makes me miss huge chunks of my life that I'll never have back. There's a reason so many religious and spiritual paths pray and meditate and focus on freeing themselves from the seductive storylines of the self-cherishing mind.

I spent some time looking into these practices and what I noticed was that if I just had one voice chattering away up there I might stand some sort of chance of getting control over it, but the truth is, I have a whole committee of voices and characters that live in my head, and they all have very different agendas. They all have strong attachments to certain things which must happen and other things which mustn't happen, and they don't all match up. How are we supposed to move forward gracefully with our projects and relationships when part of us wants to go left and another equally vital part of us wants to go right? It's no wonder we often go around in circles.

One character in my mind says, 'If only we had more money. Life would be so much better if I had loads of money,' and there's another one in there who thinks, 'Aren't rich people wankers?' Conflicting needs, conflicting perspectives, and both of them me. We are giving ourselves mixed messages and it can be impossible to satisfy the whole committee that lives in my head.

These characters are never going away, they are with us for life, and when left to their own devices they can be confusing and demotivating, even destructive. They become so troublesome and unruly that we call them demons, but are they all trouble or might they have essential gifts for us? Perhaps it's all in the framing.

DAEMONS VS DEMONS

In the good old days back in Ancient Greece 'daemons' were divine helpers rather than problems. The Romans called this kind of attendant spirit 'genius', so rather than an individual being a genius, the genius was a divine entity that was believed to live in the walls of the artist's studio and would come out and assist or inspire in their creativity. Your daemon was your friend, a sort of semi-magical being who lived half in this world and half in the spirit world, unbound by the same earthy laws as you and I. It could run ahead down the path and warn us of approaching hazards. They were there to show us stuff. In fact, as my pal and anarchic workshop creator Dave Rock told me recently, the word 'monster' comes from the French word *'montrer'* meaning to show. Hence our word for 'demonstrate'. Long ago, if you committed a crime or indecency in France you would be dressed up as the exaggerated version of your crime and paraded around the village as a cautionary tale to others.

The early Christians were frightened of the perceived power of these daemons and so the idea spread that they were evil, looking to control human beings rather than help them. Now we've become so used to resisting the unexpected and uncomfortable things which arise that we 'demonise' them and push them away. How would it be if we harvested their jewels instead? Yes, they do leap out at often inconvenient moments, and yes, they can seem upon first inspection to be potentially destructive or chaotic, but when framed differently they can contain potent wake-up calls.

Have you seen the *Pink Panther* movies with Peter Sellers playing Inspector Clouseau? He is a bumbling French police detective who has an Asian manservant called Cato (not Catto), an expert in martial arts whose job is to attack Clouseau unexpectedly, leaping out from hiding places, to keep Clouseau's combat skills sharp. Of course he always attacks at the 'wrong moment' and Clouseau shouts, 'Not now, Cato!' as they fight and pretty much always totally trash whatever environment they're in.

Our demons are Cato. On some level we hired them to show us, not always comfortably, things we need to be aware of or be reminded of, especially our disowned self. And of course, in the surprise of their sudden appearances, leaping out of the closets of our lives, we nearly always scream, 'Not now, Cato!' – but there's an invitation to reframe and re-evaluate our demons and even transform them into illuminating allies. When we treat them as friends keeping us on our toes, not enemies hindering us, a whole new menu of opportunity is on offer.

In making a list of the primary bad guys who live in my head, the first eight or so seem pretty universal. I'm not sure I'll ever get to the end of the list, but here are some of the main players. I wonder if you have them, too.

1) The Pessimistic Worrier

Whatever's about to happen, especially something which is not in my control, there's a character who lives in my head who will imagine and play out the worst possible way it could go, the most negative scenarios that the Worrier thinks I need to prepare myself for. This even includes running imagined versions of potentially difficult conversations I need to have and inventing the most infuriating and triggery dialogue. Have you ever found yourself driving home and running one of these imagined exchanges in your mind? Have you ever found yourself getting angrier and angrier at the person you're having the imaginary argument with, all because of the script you gave them? I can sometimes drive for half an hour and arrive home with no memory of the route I took, I was so immersed in my negative imagination. Painting the future as black as it can be, is this some kind of insurance? Control? Does this character live in your head?

2) The To-Do-List Addict

No matter how many times I run through the list of all the things I have got to do, this character never rests. 'Let's just run that through one more time. First I'll do this, then I've got to do that . . . oh, and then . . .' The anxiety that not everything might get done or that I might miss something or forget something, the overwhelmingness and pressure of everything I've got to do, and all the diverse and vital tasks I have to remember to tick off the endless list, can send my mind into an involuntary loop. This is also the character who starts trawling for trouble when nothing is wrong. I'll sit back, relax, and then I'll start running through the checklist of my life, relationship, money and health, looking for problems, things to solve. Invariably I'll find something that isn't OK, that needs sorting out. It is like a perpetual sense of having gone out and left the gas on. Something must be wrong somewhere and I mean to find it, worry about it, and fixate on it instead of allowing myself to simply relax in the space where I am.

3) The Innocent Victim

Oh, the injustice! My inner innocent victim is always upset by others' lack of empathy and fairness. 'There I was, only trying to help . . .' Other people's unfair behaviour is both painful and deliciously addictive in a way, because it is so hard to let go of a situation where we are definitely in the right.

In fact, this character has its own cast of thousands living in my head because my innocent victim has to present unarguable evidence of his rightness and suffering of injustice, and that often plays out as a kind of courtroom scene in my mind where I list point by point items which prove my rightness and their clear wrongness, and everyone in the jury or in the gallery nods in agreement, equally outraged and sympathetic, understanding perfectly how utterly unfair this episode has been for me. How do they all fit up there in my head?

4) The Strategising Control Freak

It seems so important for everything to stay in control, to go the way I want it to. This character is very focused, and often anxious, running all kinds of control trips and strategies, weighing the odds, comparing probabilities, and devising plans and possibilities for me to have my own way. This character has a one-track mind and is fixated on only one outcome. He has no trust that unexpected situations might work out well for me. He sees through a tiny keyhole and yet acts as if he has all the information and knows his way is the best way, and when it looks like life has other plans he will attempt to take over and strong-arm everything back into his vision of rightness. This can often include manipulation – 'If I do this, then she'll do that . . . if I put it like this then they'll think . . .' – working out ways to say things to get the desired outcome, to control people without them ever feeling controlled. Mock innocence. *The greatest opportunities often come cloaked in disaster and if we are patient, things can unfold much better than the original plan we had.* This character has zero trust in that, can't wait and can't sit in the uncertainty.

5) The Vengeful Murderer

We each have our own personal cocktail of things which drive us so crazy that we almost want to kill whoever presses that button in us. For me, you only need to be driving too slowly in front of me when I'm in a hurry and I want to kill you, maybe have some huge crane appear and lift your car vertically off the road and throw it over a bridge with you inside, and for you to know it was karma exacted on you for your appalling, selfish driving. And in that rage surge I am so sure I am just and right. We have become so reactive and fragile. Most of us are lucky enough not (at this moment) to be living in a time where bombs are dropping all around us. Most of us do not (currently) need to walk eight hours to get clean water, yet we will ruin a whole day, or even a whole relationship, over *the tone of voice you just spoke to me in*. My injustice meter is so super-sensitive, and the surge of pain and injustice that can explode in me so overwhelming, that suddenly, in disbelief at the other person's outrageous wrongness, I want to kill that person, or at least make them suffer, and feel completely justified. The vengeful murderer can go from zero to one hundred per cent in a moment.

6) The Slave-Driver/Inner Critic

I'm not sure whether this is one character or two similar ones working in tandem, but I have never met anyone who is totally free of this undermining voice. When we were growing up, usually the way our parents and teachers delivered advice on how to succeed and get it right was with very critical and judgemental language. It became so important for us to achieve what was expected of us that we internalised the same voices to keep us on track and free from failure. Approval and success are so important to us that we feel justified in slave-driving ourselves along, and often our compassion for our fallibility is sacrificed along the way. It is only very recently that children were being taught that encouragement is even an option unless one is already succeeding.

7) The Naive Child

'This time it is going to be different!' Aw, bless this little boy who lives in me. I remember how neat my handwriting was on the first page of every new exercise book at school. I had such positive intentions that this time I was going to absorb what the teachers were saying. After all, everyone else seemed to get it. 'I'll just listen. I'll focus and listen. I can do this!' Yet pretty soon I'd be daydreaming again and spacing out, unable to take in what they were teaching, and inevitably would get in trouble for my laziness. Still I soldiered on with my well-intentioned version of studiousness – to no avail, sadly. The naive child in me can't understand why the world is so corrupt and unpredictable, and he often feels painfully powerless in the face of the current state of the planet. We want to live in a world where we can expect people to be fair and kind, and none of us want to live life looking through a cynical lens, expecting the worst, but inevitably certain people and situations are going to disappoint us. This little guy, like a faithful puppy, comes back again and again for more and often forgets to make the necessary boundaries I need to protect myself from the unpredictability of life's relationships and challenges.

8) The Needy One

Some people have done a great job of shutting this character down, especially as it is one of the more shameful ones, but not me. The needy one in me thinks that he depends on other people's actions and decisions to feel OK. I live in a very volatile and tenuous realm when this character is in the driving seat. The beliefs that this character lives by are totally self-sabotaging because none of us can depend on everyone else acting as we would prefer. People are undependable. Everyone has their own lives and changing priorities, and while I am only OK when they choose what I want them to choose I am guaranteed to live like a hungry ghost, never fully satisfied and never feeling fully safe. The beliefs this character lives by are rooted in childhood and can be hard to shift. To cultivate the healthy path of self-care, not dependent on others, is a wonderful yet challenging undertaking. I'm not sure the path ever ends but until I take a more self-caring attitude I can live a totally disempowered existence, as if I'm a regressed child waiting for Mother's milk. This character also brings a lot of shame with it, as our culture looks down on neediness. As Woody Allen said, 'If only neediness and begging were attractive qualities.'

9) The Flaming Sex Maniac

Anyone not have this one? Some days nearly any stimulus can trigger sexual thoughts and sometimes in the most inappropriate of situations. This character only sees life from one single perspective. When he's walking down the street all he sees are *fuckable*, *competitor* and *irrelevant*. This is one of the characters who we tend to try and keep the most hidden, as

not everyone would appreciate the nuances of our dark appetites. Our culture is very hung up around sex. As Gabrielle
Roth says, 'We make it both too important and not important
enough', and it is no radical news to suggest that religion has
been largely responsible for brainwashing generations of hell-
fearers away from their natural, horny impulses. Sexuality can
be one of the most powerful portals to experiencing one's
spirituality, to making a direct connection with whatever your
idea of the Divine is. Priests don't want to give up their jobs
of being the middle-men, so over the years they've rebranded
sex as a sinful thing and, as we said earlier, the further you
push a beach ball down under the surface of the swimming
pool the more violently it springs back up. Suppression magnifies intensity and it tends to leak out in all sorts of directions.
We probably wouldn't have the endless menu of sexual flavours
and depravities available to us had religion not been so busy
trying to ban it. That's my kind of karma!

DEMON GROUP THERAPY

When you use the Way to conquer the world,
Your demons will lose their power to harm.
It is not that they lose their power as such,
But that they will not harm others;
Because they will not harm others,
You will not harm others:
When neither you nor your demons can do harm,
You will be at peace with them.

Tao de Ching

These living characters have needs and fears and compulsions. When we are in constant shame and suppression of these essential parts of ourselves, our demons find their own ways to get their needs met, and often in unexpectedly dramatic and self-sabotaging ways. These characters never die (until we do) and they need expression, so if we don't feed meat to the demons we are setting ourselves up for endless unexpected dramas. We need to enter into a new relationship with these guys and stop trying unsuccessfully to hide them in the basement. They start banging on the trap door and as Tom Robbins says, 'In the darkness they grow fangs and at unexpected moments leap out and bite you'. We almost need to start our day with a little group therapy session with the characters in our heads.

Ah, good morning, murderer, who's on the list today? Oh, everyone? OK . . . and, sex maniac, what is it today? Oh, donkeys and baked beans, nice.

Once their desires are given a little oxygen they no longer need to force their way to the surface, breaking down the doors to get their needs met. I think of my demons as a school bus full of unruly freaks. If I don't let them express themselves they find a way to distract me and grab the wheel! 'Hey, Jamie, that guy on the internet called you a wanker!' and my attention is momentarily diverted. It only takes a second for that character to leap into the driving seat and get control of the wheel, and God help me if he gets control of the mouth or the internet. Suddenly my inner vengeful murderer has control of my email . . . arrrgh! This is truly hazardous. This is one of the areas where our faster-is-better culture really does not serve us. In the days before the internet, if I was going to write something irretrievably rude or aggressive, by the time I'd hand-written the letter, folded it and slipped it into the envelope, there's a good chance that while licking the gum I might come to my senses, crumple up the letter and write something less petulant and destructive. Email does not afford us this luxury. All too quickly I write my confrontational reply, probably totally over-reacting to whatever I have been sent as my *I'm not being treated with the respect I deserve* buttons have been pressed, I hit 'send' and it's over, another bridge burnt.

The truth is that when we stop looking at these characters as enemies and consider that there may be some benefit to reframing our experience of them there's an endless harvest of treasure available. That's right, I'm saying that even these demonic voices have a function in Life's genius. They have illuminations within, they can show us our limiting, wounded beliefs about ourselves, they can lead us into compassion for ourselves and others, and they each have skills and gifts which may presently be applied for dysfunctional ends, but with a new dialogue they can be transformed into allies, even employees. But first, we need to be willing to step into the shadows.

CHAPTER 3

Willing to Feel

Be brave enough to live life creatively. The creative is the place where no one else has ever been. You have to leave the city of your comfort and go into the wilderness of your intuition. You can't get there by bus, only by hard work and risk and by not quite knowing what you are doing. What you'll discover will be wonderful. What you'll discover will be yourself.

Alan Alda

One of the limiting habits we have formed as a species is always try to and move towards comfort and push away discomfort. We feel a pain and we take a pill to make it go away, but as long as we are always trying to escape the uncomfortable we are missing half of the treasure of life. It is when we are uncomfortable that we have to reach out to others; it cultivates intimacy and trust. When we are in pain our compassion for others who are experiencing pain, too, is deeply felt, unlike the rest of the time when we are buzzing around in self-involved busyness. The dark night of the soul is one of the most growing experiences many of us ever have.

In Eckhart Tolle's classic self-help book *The Power of Now* he talks about a concept which he calls 'the pain body'. The idea is that as we grow up, our rage and our pain and our grief are often unsupported and unwelcome in our homes and schools, and much of the time we have to suppress, not express, how we feel. When we do this, remnants of that unexpressed emotion get lodged in our bodies. Week after month after year of continually not expressing these painful cries and wounds results in an accumulation of unexpressed, over-reactive emotion in us, like a large constipated lump. This is what Tolle calls 'the pain body', and it causes us to over-react to the challenging people and experiences we encounter every day. When someone upsets us, our reaction often bears no proportional resemblance to the size of the infraction we've suffered. Why? Because we are not only feeling the pain caused in that one moment, we are experiencing the pain body rearing up with the lineage of all the times someone treated us like that, back to our early childhood. All the unexpressed times when we were hurt or unjustly treated wake up, and we howl with decades of accumulated pain. It is so overwhelmingly painful that our mind holds the person who triggered us responsible for how we are feeling, and we attack or control or condemn them, trying anything to avoid feeling the accumulated pain fully.

We each have in us a unique cocktail of accumulated, unexpressed pain influencing how we react, and we all react to different triggers. Someone who upsets you might be totally benign to me, and the guy who makes me want to explode might be just vaguely annoying to you. No matter who we are, if we grew up in a home where our natural, total expression of all our hurts was unwelcome, we will each carry our own uniquely sensitive lump of unexpressed, constipated emotional gunk, usually, in my experience, lodged down our fronts from our throat to our belly. When it is triggered the contraction that happens in our body is so excruciating that we will do anything not to feel it.

This brings us back to how our bodies are hard-wired to constantly mend themselves. Yes, when we scratch our skin it heals over, and when we break a bone it magically reknits itself, but the body is even more genius than that. It knows it has this yucky, constipated lump of over-reactive emotional 'stuff' lodged in its torso and so is understandably on a daily mission to flush that shit out.

It is almost as if each annoying experience is tailor-made to awaken a lump of that pain body so that it starts to feel itself intensely, and if we are skilful we can participate in the body/ mind's genius process of clearing out that day's cupful of emotional gunk. If we resist and control and suppress that feeling, then it gets pushed back under, waiting for another day, another trigger, to give it a chance to release. But if we are willing to feel, we have a chance, day by day, cupful by cupful, to allow Life's genius to move it all through. From this perspective, the challenging people and trigger situations of our lives are really walking laxatives sent to help us discharge all that emotional constipation.

ASTRAL ANUSES

In ancient China the dominant philosophical principle from around the fourth century BCE was the Tao, which roughly translates as the Way. They weren't busy worshipping anything or anyone but they were scientifically, and meticulously, generation by generation, mapping the pathways that this life force (Chi) moves around our bodies. To give you an example of what we mean by Chi, think of an apple that's just been picked from the tree. When you first hold it in your hand it is firm, full of juice, full of life, full of Chi, but if you leave it on the table for a couple of weeks you will see its skin begin to sag and its firmness soften as gradually all its Chi leaks out of it. The human body is the same. Early in life we are full of Chi, our skin is tight and supple, we have lots of energy, and we heal quickly, but later on as we reach old age we have far less Chi and our skin is beginning to wrinkle and sag, our self-healing capacity is drastically reduced, and our ability to leap around withers year by year.

The ancient Chinese developed systems to cultivate lots of life force and came up with methods to make sure you waste the minimum amount of it as you go through your life, so that you can meet old age with more ease and longevity. Practices they developed such as Tai Chi (literally meaning 'Big Chi') and Chi Kung are becoming more and more popular here in the West for facilitating health and wellbeing. It is not only keeping the body healthy that conserves and cultivates Chi; the way we think plays a significant role. If we are relaxed and calm we don't waste so much Chi, but if we are hectic and constantly upsetting ourselves with inner and outer conflicts, we use up our reserves of Chi and end up exhausted and depressed.

The Taoists taught that the ability to be mindful of all this and to, above all, be aware and present with how we are breathing, is the key to conserving and cultivating our life force and living a healthier and more contented life. They have all kinds of practices where when you feel into yourself, you can sense that your stomach is feeling blocked or your throat is feeling tight and you can participate with the body's genius in releasing any blockages so that the Chi can flow smoothly and unhindered around its pathways. All illnesses, the ancient Taoists believed, are the result of blockages in the complex Chi pathways of the body. Have you ever had acupuncture or seen the acupuncture map of all those pathways? Those are the major and minor Chi channels that the life force travels along, and Chinese medicine is all about helping it flow correctly to keep you well. Here is a big difference between Eastern and Western medicine. In Western medicine, we go and see a doctor only when something's gone wrong, but in China you see your doctor regularly to prevent getting ill in the first place.

In order to fully participate in this genius yet delicate process of release and unblocking we need to turn our attention inward and get to know how the insides of our bodies feel. We are used to doing this when we have sex. We can easily put our minds between our legs or wherever the pleasure is pulsing, and if we stub our toe or have a headache, it's not hard to place our attention where the painful sensation is being felt. The extension of this is not only to notice the feelings inside our bodies when they are as intense as that but to be in daily intimate contact with the subtler sensations within us and play an active role in assisting the body's genius in keeping the life force constantly unclogging itself and flowing smoothly.

Check in with your Body

In the next chapter, Full Body Listening, we'll go deeper into the specifics of how to do this, but for now just feel your whole body, wriggle your fingers, wriggle your toes, and feel how you inhabit this whole body from crown to toe, not just living solely in your head with all its busy thinking mind and chattering mouth. We are so head-centric here in the West that we often get so top-heavy we forget that our whole body is a sensitive, sophisticated feeling system that is working for us constantly, communicating and transmitting vast amounts of vital data. How does each part of your body feel right now? Don't analyse the sensations, simply observe them with gentle curiosity.

THE TRIGGER IS NOT THE CAUSE

When we begin to look at the challenging people and upsetting situations in our lives, without playing the victim and instead from the perspective that Life's genius might be doing something benevolent, we can notice two great benefits available from these. The first is that we begin to see that no matter what anyone does to us, the emotional feelings that erupt in our bodies have not been put there by the trigger. The emotional reaction comes from that old, reactive pain body which has been waiting like a silent time bomb to explode.

Here's the proof: if someone came into this room now and started being incredibly racist, I mean really going for it with all the forbidden words and angry, ignorant rhetoric, and you and I were standing here, I might have a total emotional meltdown and start freaking out while you might acknowledge they're a racist and be repelled by them but not go into the same total emotional freakout as me. What does this tell us? We have both been exposed to exactly the same stimulus. I'm melting down and reacting very dramatically, and you, while still acknowledging they're a crazy bigot, are emotionally calm. That's because I already carry a dormant, reactive time bomb from my past experiences with racists, or from other violent people, and you do not. The emotionally reactive potential is in me, and although the racist might have triggered my time bomb to go off painfully, he didn't cause it. That distinction is vital if we are going to take mature responsibility for the reactive parts of ourselves that go off in us day after day. The trigger is *not* the cause. No one can send us into an emotional tailspin if we don't already have an Achilles' heel in that area. So if I acknowledge that although the racist may definitely be wrong and bad and his behaviour inexcusable, the following reaction that I'm experiencing in my body came from my own uniquely reactive potential that lives in my tender pain body. I have that flavour of reactivity in me just waiting to get triggered by a racist, and you do not. My reaction is mine.

It is incredibly seductive to believe that whoever wronged us is responsible for the painful reaction we feel, but it is a mistake which often distracts us from meeting this experience with power and wisdom. I have just been vividly made aware of one of the reactive time bombs that lives in my body. Could it be that once again Life's genius is helping me? If I have the balls (or ovaries) to step out of my victim-led take on what just happened and meet the experience with the full potential that's on offer here, I will be almost grateful for what just happened. It is signalling to me that I have something I have been carrying around all this

to dissolve in my body. With my breath and
e a chance to go internal and fully feel the erup-
nect from the external stimulus that set it off.

Now   not to say that it won't be appropriate to have a
sober conversation with whoever hurt me, but if I don't take
space and first address the painful eruption in my body then
when I immediately confront the trigger person I will invariably
sink deeper into a fight, and my over-reaction will usually set
off their reactive side. If I go straight into battle with the trigger
I'll be doing it as a way to abandon my own feelings, and to use
that person to avoid myself.

If I first address and dissolve the charge in my body and only
then have the conversation with the trigger person then I will
not be coming at them with angry blame and leaking my rage
all over them. If I let the charge in me settle down first, then
there's a real chance that the person I need to set boundaries
with, or share my needs or judgements with, will actually hear
me, and my calmer, more responsible demeanour will elicit a
calmer and more grounded response.

> Between the stimulus and the response there's a space, and
> in that space is our power and our freedom.
>
> Victor Frankl

DISSOLVING EMOTION

Returning to the ancient Chinese Taoists, we can see what
dissolving the reaction might look like. They discovered thousands of years ago that by placing your attention in the area where

the eruption is being felt, and by breathing gently there, by creating an idea of spaciousness around the sensations and willingly feeling all the sensations, instead of the usual practice of avoiding the feeling and battling the external, then with patience and even friendliness, the painful blockage begins to dissolve, your nervous system calms down, and a thimbleful of your reactive constipation is discharged. This might be in the form of some emotion being felt, or just the pressure easing and moving out of the body.

Usually, when someone irritates us, instead of responsibly going internal, we go straight into battle with the external stimulus to make the feeling go away. We argue with them, we condemn, we manipulate, we numb ourselves out or escape in a number of ways – anything but feel the feeling fully in our bodies. We need to totally turn this habit around if we are to be free and creative in the world. Instead of rejecting those painful feelings, we need to turn our attention away from the external and go inward. Instead of trying not to feel what erupted in us, we need to become fascinated with it, willing to feel every atom of it. We become like a wine-taster, a connoisseur alert to the tiniest sensations within the pain body. This is how to be a willing participant with what Life's genius is offering us at that moment. It is only by feeling these waves fully with total willingness that they get to find their expression, be fully felt, and then dissolve from our bodies for ever. When we make a committed practice of using the painful triggers of life in this way then we don't need to keep encountering the same shit day after day. There is progress, and we gradually learn to accept and welcome all our feelings as useful conduits to free ourselves from the tyranny of our reactions. When I fight the external, I am a slave. When I am willing to feel, I am powerful.

If someone comes along and shoots an arrow into your
heart, it is fruitless to stand there and yell at the person.
It would be much better to turn your attention to the fact
that there's an arrow in your heart.

Pema Chödrön

Our physical reactions to stories or events from the past, or from
things which are unfolding right now, when fully felt, willingly,
have a place in our bodies. You can ask: 'Is it in my solar plexus?'
'Is my chest tightening?' When we give it some attention it
becomes obvious where in the body the 'blockage' is lodged.
These disruptive events or challenges can be useful signposts to
locate the nooks and crannies of stale and stuck emotion. It is
useful to sometimes drum up that story, let the events and possibilities that bother us come to mind, and then immediately feel
where in our body a sensation has been activated. Bingo! It is
like an FBI phone-tapping device. The story leads me to the
feeling like a tracking mechanism and betrays the hiding places
of the blockage.

For example, when my girlfriend talks to me in a certain tone
of voice I can feel an angry tightness rising in me. It starts in
my legs, it enters my breath and chest, and can trigger a dispro-
portionately dramatic rage reaction in me if I don't notice it in
time. The accumulation of all the times my mother spoke to
me like that and I felt unseen or misjudged is still living in
me, and the similarity of my partner, who is usually totally
innocently observing something, challenging me or pointing
something out, awakens all the unexpressed rage and claustro-
phobia of my past. At this moment I have a choice: I can spill
years of undischarged bile all over her, blame her and reject her

and hold her responsible for the horrid feeling I'm experiencing, *or*, if I am skilful and brave, I can turn inward, notice the massive volcano erupting in me, choose not to make it her fault but take full responsibility for it. In practice this would mean taking some space to breathe through and dissolve or discharge the sensation before I unskilfully fall into a row with her and end up sleeping on the sofa. Even better, to vulnerably express to her what I'm going through without making it her fault or triggering her into defensiveness is the real black-belt way to respond because then I can receive her support and gentle head stroking or holding while I process it, and it can be a route to a deepening of our intimacy. This is, to me, alchemy, transforming what could have been shit into relationship gold.

It is ironic, really, because we spend so much of our time worried about being abandoned or exiled in different ways, but, truthfully, whenever we try and battle or manipulate the external to avoid feeling these painful reactions, it is like we are saying to ourselves, 'These feelings are not OK to feel, your feelings are not welcome!' We are abandoning ourselves. No one else can abandon us if we are willing to feel all our feelings. So when, for example, we are hoping that our partner won't abandon us, we are really looking in the wrong place. It is no one else's job to make us feel safe. Yes, we can set up safe agreements and boundaries for ourselves, and hopefully the people we love will agree to them, but it is not their job to be scaffolding for our soul. They can support us and they can be there in the hard times, but it is no one else's job to notice how we are feeling and make sure our emotional needs are met, and it is also a massive turn-off for a lover to be expected to be our parent or carer. They don't have the capacity to guarantee to us that they'll never ever leave. The only person that can guarantee to me that they'll never ever abandon me is *me*.

DISSOLVING UNDERLYING BELIEFS

The second opportunity that Life's genius is offering us when we are triggered is to discover what beliefs we are carrying that keep these kinds of reactions repeating and repeating. We never feel stressed or reactive about something unless we have a belief running inside us that holds the feeling in place.

Someone who has made a whole system for this kind of enquiry is an American teacher called Byron Katie. She has a sophisticated yet simple and effective method for going into these beliefs and dissolving them (www.thework.com). The first thing she asks is: 'Is the belief definitely true?' And we often discover, time after time, that it isn't and that we have a choice as to whether we want to habitually keep believing it or whether we can let it go.

For instance, I have always been a needy, abandonment-phobic kind of a boyfriend (or husband). If I sense or suspect that my partner is attracted to someone else, internally I start tightening up and waves of anxiety begin to course through me. If I have more evidence of my partner being attracted to another man, I will likely surrender to excruciatingly jealous feelings and thoughts. Why?

What would I have to believe is true to feel this way about this?

I asked that question and I realised, wow, I would have to believe that if she left me for someone else my life would be unliveable, and in that moment I became powerful again, because it was then up to me to go deeper into the belief, maybe consider where and when it was implanted, and then choose not to live by its false projections (until next time – it can take a bit of practice!).

Fear is really such a blessing because it gives us a menu of the beliefs we are carrying that aren't true for us any more. Of course there are some genuine survival issues in life that we do need to be afraid of, but most of our head-fucking about what might happen is a total waste of energy. As Mark Twain said, 'I have lived through some terrible things in my life – some of which actually came to pass.'

If I go deeper into my beliefs I notice that somewhere deep down inside I believe that if my partner ever left me for another man then my life would be unliveable. It would be over. If I am holding that belief to be true, then when there is any kind of a threat or suspicion my body will react as if life is literally falling apart. I am so sure that life would be unliveable if she left me that if anything signals that possibility I begin to melt down. But is that belief really true? Yes, if she left me for someone else it would be really painful, maybe even hellish for a time, but for how long really? A few months maybe? Even if it was, in drastic circumstances, a whole year, before very long I would get over it and meet someone else.

Most of us have been in relationships that ended and we are all still here getting on with our lives, in new relationships or open to whatever is coming around the next corner. Very few of us died from a broken heart, but we (well, OK, I) act as if being left for another lover would literally kill us. So the second invitation which is on offer from the painful feelings that go off in our bodies is to enquire into the belief that is holding that reaction in place and to see, with a little scrutiny, whether that belief is actually true.

We usually reject feelings of fear. Of course, they don't feel comfortable, but Bashar invites us to look at them differently. He says that fear is the same energy as excitement going through our body but bumping into beliefs that are not in alignment with who we really are, so although it can be painful, it is also a signpost. He says that when you play the piano and hit an out-of-tune note, you don't run away from the piano and swear never to play it again; you tune the note. Fear is telling us where we have an out-of-tune belief that needs dissolving, so we could actually get excited about it. Wow, a fear, how exciting! I can dissolve something holding me back!

WILLING TO FEEL

They say that you can't love anyone until you love yourself, but what does self-love mean? What does it entail? I mean, I bought some chamomile tea, does that count? Self-love begins with the willingness to feel all our feelings without rejecting our own experience, not by abandoning the young character who lives in us, but by welcoming the waves as much as possible and reminding ourselves that all our feelings are OK to feel. If I go soft and yield to it.

This is where the masculine side of our nature has to take a back seat. It is not about analysing the feeling or doing something to make it go away, it is not about taking any action. It is the feminine part of us that is most useful here. The part of us that gets impacted, that can allow the sensations deeper in. Every time we make space to feel, to allow, to yield to what's happening, we send a message of self-care and acceptance to our wounded places and give them permission to exist. In this way we take one more step towards wholeness and integration and become less reliant on other people making it better for us.

When emotions arise we often try to stifle them. We mustn't cry in public, right? We don't want to be a burden on people, we don't want to look needy or as if we are trying to get attention with our drama, and our intense emotions have rarely been supported and approved of in our childhoods, so the first impulse, when tears or anger rise up, is to push them back down. The self-loving practice that has created great shifts in my life is to cry and cry and cry, not self-indulgently wallowing, but consciously feeling all my feelings, saying yes, yes, yes, as I feel each wave pass through me, and soon enough it passes and ebbs, and I feel lighter. The times when I collapsed with anxiety or panic attacks, I would notice a pressure in my chest, the pressure of years of corked tears.

Once when I was sixteen, I was having such an intense meltdown that I called the doctor. An hour later I was sitting in his waiting room and a sudden surging of emotion took me by surprise. The tears burst out of me and I cried for about ten minutes. After the wave had passed I noticed that the panic attack had totally vanished. I sat there feeling absolutely fine and a little bit sheepish. I didn't have anything to show the doctor any more. I got up and slipped out of the waiting room and went home.

Now I cry often. It feels good, like doing a huge poo. Sometimes it is from sorrow welling up, sometimes from sudden beauty or intimacy. I let myself weep in public places and alone driving in the car. My body wants to love itself this way. I'm glad I don't suppress it any more.

This being human is a guest house. Every morning a new arrival. A joy, a depression, a meanness, some momentary awareness comes as an unexpected visitor. Welcome and attend them all! Even if they're a crowd of sorrows, who violently sweep your house empty of its furniture, still treat each guest honourably. He may be clearing you out for some new delight. The dark thought, the shame, the malice, meet them at the door laughing, and invite them in.

Rumi

THE ART OF RECEIVING

If you're someone who'd like to take the journey to feeling all of your own feelings and being less reliant on the artists to deliver a placebo version for you, then developing the ability to drop into your more feminine, allowing, melting nature is essential. When I say feminine I don't mean womanly. Each of us, men and women, have both feminine and masculine aspects within us, what the ancient Chinese called Yin and Yang. The masculine in us is the quality that goes out into the world, that gives, that penetrates, that acts, that gets busy 'doing' in the world. The feminine part of us is the aspect in us which listens, which receives and is penetrated by life. The feminine is more about feeling things and the masculine is more about doing things.

When we surrender to our more feminine aspect, the worry is that we will be totally taken over by the experience and that somehow we might lose ourselves and never come back, as if we are going to drown in the endless ocean of it all, but the truth is we only experience these vulnerable waves one at a time. Even if some of the waves are big and crash down on our rocks, no one is expected to experience the whole ocean all at once. We only ever have to experience the sensation of each moment at a time, not our whole lifetime of depression or terror. Often we are so afraid of our feelings because we feel the whole weight of that pain, the whole unmanageable idea of it that makes us feel help-less, but all pain, when reduced to just this solitary moment's experience of it, is actually something we can handle. Just this one moment of it. The greatest advice I ever heard given to women giving birth is that you don't have to experience all the contractions all at once, only each one at a time. When you look at childbirth as hours and hours of painful contractions it seems an impossible task, but when you realise that you only have to feel through this one contraction then it becomes manageable, step by step.

The most helpful technique I have learned to allow myself gradually to stop resisting the more uncomfortable waves of intensity that life serves me up is to focus only on the feeling of this exact moment, which is really all I am ever asked to do. I don't have to feel all the depression or anxiety ahead, only this single moment. This has really helped me.

Can I handle feeling this sensation in my body in just this moment? . . . Yes

Can I handle feeling this sensation in my body in just this moment? . . . Yes

Can I handle feeling this sensation in my body in just this moment? . . . Yes

As in drug-addiction rehab therapy where they say just make it through this day without using drugs, this practice is like a micro moment-by-moment version of that. Just make it through this moment, and leave the next one until it arrives in the Now. You can only experience anything in the Now, in the present moment; anything else is a painful abstraction. We can't feel future pain, only what is passing through us in the present moment and pretty much all present moments are handleable (if only just).

It is often the idea of the pain that is hurting us, not the sensations themselves, but when I allow my mind to get less busy creating meanings and stories about the pain and instead just feel the purely physical sensations of it, it is much more manageable. This is a lesson from Vipassana meditation, in the Buddhist tradition: to focus just on the physical sensations and remove the labels. When intense feelings are moving through, it is not always helpful to attach our usual labels to what we are feeling. We are used to calling it 'grief' or 'loss' or 'anxiety', but this can be a distraction, and the labels can limit the experience by connecting it to all the aversions we have to those words. The words associated with intense feelings are usually so negative that they trigger immediate resistance, but when I remove all labels from the feeling and just experience it as a wave with no name, it moves through me with less drama.

Another trap to watch out for while we are feeling ourselves so fully and dissolving our blockages is the over-personalisation of what's going on. Focusing on it being my pain, my demons, my depression, can isolate us from the support of the shared human experience. It can be really helpful in these moments to imagine, right now, there's a man setting up his fruit stand in Peru who's feeling just like this. There's a woman walking her dog in Paris who's feeling just like this. There's a kid lying in bed in America who's feeling just like this. Maybe I'm not feeling my sadness. Maybe I'm feeling *the* sadness. Perhaps we are all given a bucketful of pain to process in our lifetimes which is everyone's, and we each carry our share.

I love how the Tibetan Buddhists do their dissolving practice. They call it Tonglen, and after they've done their breathing and dissolving of the blocked emotion, as a last stage they say: 'May this practice help all beings who are feeling like this be free from suffering.'

I love that.

Try this experiment when you next have a headache. Of course the usual thing is to take a pill and make it go away. It is a headache after all, an ache, an unwanted thing that should be got rid of, right? But what if we remove the accustomed framing of the experience from the usual negative labelling and just let it be a neutral experience? How weird would it be to become fascinated with the feeling of it? Try it. Go deeper into it. Where exactly is it? In the skull? In the eyes? How big is it? What colour is it? What texture is it? You'll be amazed that when you do this it begins to morph and change. Keep asking those questions round and round, and watch the sensation as a fascinated observer, a botanist making sketches and notes on a rare new insect or flower. It keeps changing, it feels different, it moves . . . and . . . oh . . . it is gone. Once again, by willingly choosing to feel whatever's going on to its absolute fullest, we allow the body/mind genius to do what it is best at: discharging and redistributing blockages. And all this without the need to rely on a chemical drug manufactured by a multinational pharmaceutical company with no interest in you or your body's health.

The Buddhists teach us to leave the back door open and the front door open. Feelings come in the back door but we don't attach to them, label them, get busy analysing them. We don't make them a cup of tea, we simply allow them to come in the back door and pass out the front door unhindered.

No one gets to live a life without melancholy; it is an essential part of our humanity. It can feel insecure and wobbly when it arises, but this is the moment when we have to stop . . . listen . . . feel . . . and ask ourselves what is the most self-caring option available to us in that moment. It is easy to turn habitually to one of our addictions at that moment, switch on the TV or go on Facebook, take a drink or a drug to numb the feeling, make a journey to the fridge or have a wank, do something to change what's going on in ourselves, but if I am opting for the more self-loving and self-caring path I will pause for a moment and have enough intimacy with myself to ask the golden question: *What do I need right now?*

Instead of escaping into addiction, perhaps sit under a tree and write a poem or call a friend or get into nature. Our feelings are asking us to take care of ourselves and when we frame our lives this way we often start creating our best art and experiencing a more nourishing depth to our relationships.

Pain + Resistance = Suffering
Pain + Willingness = Liberation

This practice isn't limited to the uncomfortable feelings. Our inspirations and excitements need to be listened to as well. For me, the most dependable data for trusting which action to take or inspiration to follow is listening to the attraction and excitement in my body. Excitement is the compass of my life and informs me, when I give myself space to listen, which path will be the most fulfilling and beneficial. Yes, it can be vulnerable to trust that compass but it has never led me wrong. Often some fear-based 'what ifs' will arise, like money worries or what others may think of me if I choose this, but I believe Life is signalling to me through my feelings and when I trust them, even though the outcomes are often unexpected, I usually end up somewhere inspiring and illuminating.

> For a seed to achieve its greatest expression, it must come completely undone. The shell cracks, its insides come out and everything changes. To someone who doesn't understand growth, it would look like complete destruction.
>
> Cynthia Occelli

CHAPTER 4

Full Body Listening

There is something strange going on here. Something out of the ordinary. I feel it less with my mind than my whole body.

Haruki Murakami, *IQ84*

When I write a song, I don't use my linear masculine mind to *think up* a song, rather I sink back into my more feminine, receptive aspect and twiddle around on the guitar, humming abstractly, listening and listening, and if I am lucky I might *hear* a melody. When that happens I quickly grab a pen and write it down, but the inspiration that arrived was not *thought up* or devised by my masculine, thinking mind. It was more received, from who knows where, as if my creativity were an aerial, a receiving device that picked it up from somewhere beyond my brain, or deep in my unconscious.

As I have discussed, the way we are trained in our early years massively favours the more masculine, academic, cerebral and linear sides of our decision making and barely gives a nod to the feminine in each of us, which listens, receives, yields and can allow itself to be impacted. We've been trained to fill the space with thinking and strategising, not drop into space and discover what arises from the void. And yet my own creative and emotional life has proved to me over and over again how it is this *listening* side of my nature that delivers the great inspirations of my life and the possibility of one of my projects achieving something truly special. We can be forgiven for believing that it is our mental capacities that are able to deliver the best results; after all, it's how we have been taught all the way through our education. The mind will usually come up with a 67.5% good plan for anything we apply it to (that's a B+), and so we will settle for that and think it is our best option, but when we dare to allow the greater resource that is available beyond the limitations of the mind's strategies, something unexpectedly genius can be sourced with much less effort, and all we have to do is write it down and take the money and the credit.

No one has ever been able to discover fully where inspiration comes from. Most writers and artists I know are comfortable with it being a mystery, but one thing we all agree on is that, wherever it is sourced, if we want to bring in a Masterpiece we have to make ourselves available for it. We have to find a way to enter a space where the mysterious muses can reach us.

There is a great example of this in C.S. Lewis's book *The Screwtape Letters*. C.S. Lewis was a wonderful, mystical thinker and *The Screwtape Letters* is a series of letters from an old devil to a young devil on how best to tempt the human that he has been assigned to. It's hilarious. The part that has always stayed with me is when the uncle devil instructs his nephew, Wormwood, not to worry that his human is doing so much praying. He tells him that as long as the man keeps talking to God and apologising to God and asking

God for things, as long as the words and thoughts are going in the direction from the man's mouth up towards God, then the devils have nothing to worry about. It is only when the man goes quiet and becomes empty, and allows God's love to come down from above into him, which, he says, as anyone knows, is the only true form of prayer, only then do they know the devils have a problem.

Leaving space and entering the listening field is the optimum way to access the potent inspirational forces outside our vastly limited human brain's capacity. It is why the symbol of the Holy Chalice is so fundamental to Christian mysticism. A cup is an empty vessel that can be filled up by the love of the Divine. Opening up to be poured into is what receiving the Holy Spirit is all about. The quest for the Holy Grail is not about going out to find an actual cup (though it's typical of the early Christians to totally misunderstand the point); it is about you yourself *being the cup*. I am the chalice ready to be filled with inspiration when I empty myself of all my preconceptions and surrender to what is flowing into me.

All the most juicy and fulfilling experiences of my life are rooted in the listening field. Think of when your best friend is heartbroken and you are holding space for them. You love them, so you are really present with them, really listening, and then suddenly out of your mouth comes some genius, compassionate insight and you think, wow, where did that come from? I am fucking deep today! It arose from your deep, listening field, from a place that I believe lies beyond the linear, thinking part of your mind. All the best lovemaking happens in the listening field when your whole body is intuitive and sensitive to your partner. All the best parenting happens in the listening field, tuning in to what your kids are feeling behind their words and actions. All the best creating happens in the listening field when you allow space for the muse to visit.

Listen beyond Words

Rudolf Steiner, in his book *Knowledge of the Higher Worlds and Its Attainment*, suggests a meditation that cultivates the essence of this practice beautifully. He says that when you listen to a dog barking or a baby crying, first just listen to the sound of the barking or the crying, but then see if you can tune in to the impulse that threw that sound out. See if you can listen to what was the energy that made that sound spring forth before it became a sound? In this way of listening beneath the surface we get a much truer and richer experience of the things people express to us. Have you ever had the experience of hearing someone talking and you think, 'they are saying this but really what I'm getting is that'? We all experience that natural sense of intuition when we listen a bit deeper.

This isn't, perhaps, how we usually listen. Have you noticed when you are in conversation with someone and they say something interesting that makes you remember something fascinating to add to what they have just said? At that moment we stop listening so attentively and instead hold on to the thing we want to add, just waiting for a pause or a breath to insert our offering, and the quality and depth of our listening goes out the window. The desire to impose our own angle and to be heard drastically reduces our ability to be as present with this person as we were a moment ago. This isn't listening any more. It's waiting, while we half listen, so that we can insert ourselves into the space.

The composer Debussy put it beautifully when he said, 'Music is the space between the notes'. We get a truer version of things when we focus on the space as much as the content. If you want to see this in action, there's an excellent book called *Drawing on the Right Side of the Brain* by Betty Edwards. In it, Edwards suggests that when we are drawing something such as a hand, if we focus on the fingers and thumb when we are sketching, because our brains already have such a specific idea of what a finger or a thumb looks like, by the time our eyes have left the image of the hand we are drawing when our pencil touches the paper we are already drawing an image of a hand which is totally influenced by what our memory tells us a hand should look like, rather than the hand in front of us. The resulting image often ends up unsatisfying. If instead of looking at the fingers and thumb we focus on the spaces between the fingers, and the negative space around the hand, we are much more likely to draw an accurate image. Our brain doesn't have a preconceived idea of what the triangle of negative space between the fingers should look like so when your pencil touches the paper, the space that you draw is much more faithful to the one you were just looking at.

Try drawing a hand or a chair in this way and you will be amazed at what an incredible artist you are. The same goes for forging someone's signature. If you just try and copy someone's signature as you see it on the page, somehow the results don't quite capture the character of that signature, but if you turn the signature you're copying upside down and just follow what are now abstract shapes with no concern for making anything look like letters or names, just copy the loops and angles you see, then when you turn it back around you will see a signature that truly reflects the character of the one you are forging. Once again it is the space between things that gives us the quality results we are hoping to achieve.

WU WEI

I talk a lot about the distinction between the feminine aspects of our nature and the masculine. If we return to the ancient Chinese Taoists who expressed these principles in the terms of Yin and Yang, feminine and masculine, we see how unlike our Western, male-dominated perspective their philosophy was. The Taoists had a whole wing of knowledge called Wu Wei, which means yielding to the natural way things are already flowing, or, in another way, active non-doing. How cool is that? A philosophy of deliberately leaving space, of waiting and not putting your big foot in it before whatever is going on has had time to reveal itself.

This is particularly important in business. When you are in back-and-forth negotiations with someone and there is a waiting period where you are expecting to hear their offer or their next response, it can be really challenging to sit in the fire of not yet knowing how it is going to unfold. Those who are less able to be with that feeling of uncertainty often need to reach out or make a premature phone call which betrays their lack of stead-fastness and confidence. Being unable to leave space blows many a deal, so it is usually those who can wait, who can resist making that unnecessary call, who achieve the most success.

I remember a time when I bought a car and I decided that this time I would spend a little more money and choose one that didn't break down every five minutes. Something that would last and keep going, especially as I was now driving about 2,000 miles a week to bestow my humble workshop genius upon my disciples. I had been in a transitionary period after moving back to the UK following my divorce, with no home or car, and the times when I had my kids were a bit fragmented and ungrounded.

It had been a time of cheap Travelodge roadside motels and dodgy hire cars, so by the time I rocked up to collect my daughters in my shiny new vehicle I felt like I had returned to my rightful Superdad status again. I had filled the back seat with rugs and cushions and planned a road trip to Devon for our maiden voyage. 'Come on, girls, get in, your new chariot awaits!' We set off feeling brilliant, with something appropriately victorious pumping out of the stereo speakers, and before long we were zooming along the A-roads towards the West Country, munching on biscuits and being careful not to scatter too many crumbs.

At some point though, as the road began to climb uphill, I noticed that the car wasn't feeling quite as powerful as before; in fact, it had begun to slow down. I felt that sinking feeling in my stomach. Oh no. Please. I tried to ignore it and wondered, well, maybe this is what diesel cars do when they go uphill, but as a huge juggernaut powered past me blasting its five-tone mega-horn I felt my poor Superdad-balls shrinking. Worse still, a concerned little voice asked me from the back, 'What's the matter, Daddy?' Arrrgh! It wasn't long before the rage and self-loathing kicked in. Shit! I've fucking done it again! Bollocks!

I'd only paid for the car in the last twenty-four hours and was totally within my rights to stomp straight back over there and get my money back. Then, I paused for a moment, and thought, Jamie, how about trying out just one of those things that you keep telling everyone else to do in your workshops? And so I reluctantly made no fuss or demands of the car people when I brought it back in to be looked at. I left space (growling internally but biting my tongue), and within a couple of days I received a call from the garage and it turned out that they had fixed it for free. Not only that, but when they lifted out the gearbox to diagnose the problem they found an even bigger issue which had been missed, and they ended up having to install over five thousand pounds' worth of new parts, nearly doubling its value! All this from leaving space. Had I done what I usually do and demanded my money back on the spot I would have missed the bounty. Great opportunities often come cloaked in disaster but only if we can hold on to our onions and wait and see how it unfolds. Could it be that Life's benevolent genius was trying to give me a car worth double what I paid for it?

So I tried it a second time. Later that year we were making some music for a TV station in a country where we have learned the hard way to be very careful about handing over the master tapes before getting paid. I won't mention its name (India). Anyway, we had delivered the music, and before the money came through I received an email saying that after all they didn't want thirty-second versions, they now wanted forty-second versions. That familiar *I fucking knew this would happen* feeling exploded in my chest and I had my phone in my hand within a second, looking for the number of the dastardly advertising agency who were screwing us. The studio had already been disassembled and the crew had gone home, so it wouldn't have been a totally simple matter to get it all up on the desk again to give them their new cuts of the music. Then, as my thumb hovered over the call button, that voice whispered again not to act so quickly, not to call them in this moment of self-righteous anger, but to leave space. Grrr! I didn't want to. I was right! They were wrong! This was outrageous! But I took a deep breath and laid my phone aside, imagining all the ways I would tell them how this wasn't what we had agreed. I waited. I left space, and once again the Wu Wei fairies delivered! Within an hour, a second email arrived saying that actually they wanted both thirty-second versions and forty-second versions, and everyone got paid another lump of cash on top of what we had already charged them. Leaving space resulted in Life's genius coughing up another bundle of money for everyone.

This ability to leave space is fundamental to feeling ourselves fully and letting in the great inspirations and the big ideas. It's the Yin (feminine), spacious part of us that receives the vision, and then the Yang (masculine) part of us that can spring into action, gather wood and nails and tools, and start actively building and doing and getting busy manifesting that vision here in the world. That's why, when it comes to creativity, I always have my masculine at the service to my feminine. There is no point in my manifesting and leadership qualities taking any action if they haven't first taken direction from the part of me that has received the broader vision. First, the feminine decides where we are going to go and only then does the masculine lead us there. If my masculine starts getting busy without listening and receiving first, then what I will build will usually be the product of some misguided ego-trip and not an offering from the truest, most inspired potential in me.

ACCESSING THE LISTENING FIELD

In order for us to navigate what I have been suggesting so far in this book, we need to develop a technique which I call Full Body Listening. What this means is that we learn how to be naturally in touch with the feelings and messages being felt throughout our whole bodies, from crown to toe, rather than living constantly in our heads and rarely experiencing anything from the neck down, unless there is extreme pain or pleasure going on down there. We need to become so natural at sensing when something feels blocked, or contracted, or numb, or even just not quite right, even if we don't know what it is. I'm talking about cultivating an intimacy with our insides, an ability to map the topography of our inner landscape on a daily basis so that when something acute *or* subtle is communicating to us, our first stop isn't mental analysis but a somatic feeling experience.

Earlier I talked about Taoist dissolving and how to breathe gently into areas which have erupted when we get upset, but the Taoists (both ancient and the modern practitioners) don't wait until there is a crisis to turn their attention inward. They cultivate the relationship with the messages of their bodies daily by sitting and feeling themselves from crown to toe and taking an inventory of anywhere that isn't spaciously open and flowing.

I will describe a couple of introductory Full Body Listening exercises to you here, and for more in-depth teaching the book for learning how to do this efficiently is called *The Tao of Letting Go* by Bruce Frantzis. Bruce is a Taoist Lineage Master who teaches these techniques brilliantly to Westerners. I have been lucky enough to learn from Bruce. It is one of the really cool things about how the ancient Chinese taught these practices, and how Bruce teaches in the present day, that on one level, like any teacher, they *show* you how to do the moves and direct the Chi with your mind, but, more amazingly, while they are talking and instructing, the real Taoist teachers are actually transmitting the ability to practise the techniques into you while you learn. They are literally filling you with *knowing* how to do it while you are with them. In the times I've been present with Bruce I am magically able to feel all the Chi moving around my body in a much more unmissable way than when I am doing my practice at home. Suddenly I'm quite brilliant at it! After Bruce has left the building, day by day this vicariously acquired skill does begin to fade and you have to be diligent about cultivating the sensitivity alone, making the most of the kick-start he has given you.

When it comes to their daily dissolving practice, the Taoist will sit or stand fairly straight, and similar to the Vipassana meditation practice (page 54), imagine a three-dimensional radar going from the crown of the head ever so slowly down through the body, a bit like a flat surface of water passing through the body, and whenever they discover a spot or an area which feels like it's not totally open and flowing they invite it to gently dissolve. Now, this doesn't mean they blast it with their X-ray vision like Superman. No, that would be the masculine way to do it. What the Taoists do is use their feminine essence to create space around the blockage and simply allow it to dissolve. If you want to know how to do this properly you should get Frantzis's book or audio CD, but until then, if you'd like to start the process, it is important to become conversant with the inner landscape of your body. One way I like to do this is to practise a simple Taoist meditation which is great for getting used to strolling around the inside of your body and feeling what it feels like.

INNER SMILE MEDITATION

You know how when you are driving and somebody lets you out and there's a wave and a smile, that smile can lift your whole day? It's like the smile has a feelable impact in the body.

Now, I know that Richard Dawkins hasn't invented a machine yet to measure the level of energy a smile can transmit, but I do know my experience, and certain smiles from certain people hit me and lift me right up, sometimes for the whole day. The Taoists discovered this thousands of years ago and took the idea many steps further. They generated ways to direct that smile energy into different places in their bodies, and it is one of the most healing and energising things we can do for ourselves. The particular technique that I enjoy most is the one where they smile into their major organs. Once again, the Chinese don't wait for something to go wrong with a part of their body before they look after it. They practise preventative medicine, not crisis management as we do in the West.

To smile into our organs helps them function more efficiently and promotes health and wellbeing, and, for our purposes here, it begins to train us to feel natural about moving our attention to different places inside our bodies and directing our Chi there when we need to. The five organs we are going to include in this exercise are the heart, spleen, lungs, kidneys and the liver. Most of us only ever think about our internal organs when there is something wrong with them. I mean, when was the last time you thought about your spleen? But these amazingly designed pieces of hardware are working for us day and night, keeping us healthy and energised, and allowing us to cruise around our planet having our victories and tragedies and heartbreaks, and we rarely give them a second thought. Isn't it time we offered them a bit of gratitude?

One of the really cool things I love about the Taoists is that not only were they meticulously scientific, honing their discoveries generation after generation, but they were also really lyrical and poetic about it. When they were mapping the qualities of each of the vital organs, they not only named their functions but also assigned to each of them a colour, a season, an element, a virtue and a vice. For instance, the colour of the kidneys is dark blue, its season is winter, its element is water, its virtue is gentleness, and its vice is fear. When we smile and breathe into our kidneys we allow these ideas to include themselves in a non-busy way, and we inhale gentleness into the kidneys and exhale fear as we smile into them.

SEASON	ORGAN	ELEMENT	COLOUR	OPENING	VIRTUE	VICE
WINTER	KIDNEYS	WATER	DARK BLUE	EARS	GENTLENESS	FEAR
SPRING	LIVER	WOOD	BRIGHT GREEN	EYES	KINDNESS	ANGER
SUMMER	HEART	FIRE	RED	TONGUE	LOVE	HASTE
LATE SUMMER	SPLEEN	EARTH	YELLOW	LIPS	FAIRNESS & OPENNESS	ANXIETY
AUTUMN	LUNGS	AIR	WHITE	NOSE	COURAGE	SADNESS

It is a fairly simple process to smile and breathe into our organs. We sit comfortably with our spine straight. Don't get hung up about adopting some rigid, tight-arsed posture for this. Just be comfortable and vaguely aligned, and then close your eyes and notice you are breathing. You don't need to do anything clever with the breath, just notice it passing in and out naturally. By the way, if ever you're freaking out, simply returning to the breath, noticing you are breathing in, and noticing you are breathing out, is the simplest and most effective way to come back to your calm presence and rescue your crazy mind from whatever head trip it has embarked upon.

Anyway, back to the meditation. Sit comfortably, and once you are settled in your breathing, turn the corners of your lips up at the sides so that your mouth goes into a kind of smile shape, and then allow the muscles around your face and eyes to soften, and already you may begin to notice the sensation of your inner smile bubbling up from somewhere inside you. Don't feel that you have to rush this or force it. Sometimes it is more noticeable than others – it's not a big deal – but just allow everything to go soft and smile gently with your face as you breathe. The next step is to allow the sense of smiling to enter your breath, inhaling the smile and exhaling the smile, almost creating a smile tide flowing in and out with your breathing. Already you will find your central nervous system is loving it and becoming relaxed and grounded.

Now begin to practise moving the sense of breathing around your body. It is almost like you are moving the sense of having nostrils to different places, so you start by allowing the sense of breathing to sink down to a point in the middle of your chest and imagine you are breathing in and out from that point, filling up the chest and inhaling and exhaling there for a few smiling breaths. As you do this you may feel a sensation there, a sense of warmth or energy being stimulated. Keep smiling and breathing. To take it a step further, you can allow the sense of breathing, the sense of having nostrils, to sink even lower down your body. Let your tummy go totally soft and now start inhaling and exhaling from a point about an inch below your belly button. Now you're smiling into your belly, breathing from that point a bit like a foetus does in the womb. It feels very relaxing and rooting to do this. This place in the belly that you are now breathing and smiling into is the area that the Taoists call the Lower Tan Tien, the centre of the Chi (life force) that runs through your body. It's the treasure chest where you store and generate your primary energy so it is a good area to become acquainted with.

OK, now that you are breathing and smiling, you are ready to say hello and thank you to your organs. So let's say you want to begin in the season you are in now. Depending on when you are reading this, that will vary, so I'm going to choose summer to start you off. Bring your attention and your breath to your heart and begin to appreciate how wonderful it is to have a working heart. What a wonderful machine, with its arteries and chambers, pumping away all the way through our time in the womb until our last dying breath. Breathe your smile into your heart, and as you inhale, inhale compassion, for yourself and for all living beings, all the animals and fish and birds and insects of our planet, all the beings who have come before us, all the beings who will come after us, and as you exhale, breathe out any haste or impatience or tightness that you might be carrying in your body. In with compassion, out with impatience, in with compassion, out with haste. Feel everything soften on the out breath as you appreciate your wonderful heart.

When you have done this for a minute or two, allow your attention and breath to drift down the left side of your body to the area below your bottom left rib where your spleen is. Once again, feeling appreciation for having a fully functioning spleen (whatever it does). As before, smile and breathe into it with full appreciation and gratitude, and this time as you inhale into the spleen, breathe in fairness and openness, especially to yourself, trusting Life's genius even if you can't yet see how it is all going to turn out, and as you exhale, breathe out any worry or anxiety that lives in your system, let it soften on the out breath and leave your body. In with openness, out with worry, in with fairness, out with anxiety, appreciating your functioning spleen as you smile into it, softening a little more each time.

Then, when you feel ready to move on to the next organ, allow your breath and attention to find its way to your lungs. Take a deep breath in and fill up your lungs while appreciating these incredible, oxygen-processing, self-cleaning organs. Gateways to Spirit, feel your appreciation for having two working lungs, and as you inhale and smile into them, breathe in courage, filling them up with it, and when you exhale, breathe out any grief or sadness that lives in you. Let it soften on the out breath, let it go. In with courage, out with grief, and let the out breath soften you even more each time.

Thanking your lungs one last time, now allow your attention and breath to find their way around to your lower back and your kidneys, which are either side of your mid to lower spine. Profound gratitude for having working kidneys, sophisticated water-purifying and detoxing machines, working tirelessly throughout our waking and sleeping lives. As you smile and breathe in and out of your kidneys, you may feel a response, some movement or warming. Keep smiling and breathing, and as you inhale, fill your kidneys with gentleness and on the out breath exhale any fear that lives in your body. In with gentleness, out with fear.

Last of all, allow your attention to travel to your liver, which is behind the lower ribs on your right. Again, feel the gratitude for having a working liver, this phenomenal detoxing system, and smile your breath into it gently and spaciously. As you inhale your smile into the liver, breathe in simple kindness and friendliness, filling the liver with goodwill, and as you exhale, let go of any anger or blame that is still alive in you anywhere. In with kindness, out with anger, in with friendliness, out with blame. Let any negativity in your body soften and leave on the out breath.

Now that you've said hello to your organs, you will notice that you have generated some positive or healing energy in your body, maybe even in the room where you are sitting. It is a good time now to connect to someone or somewhere outside this room that you feel could do with a healing blast of this good juice. Imagine a line connecting you to this person or place, a super cable that can take a whole river of this energy down it, and when you feel that connection, send your healing energy down the line. See the energy have its trans-formational effect in your mind's eye. That is the magic. See it rejuvenate, energise and heal. Watch a positive change occur in front of you.

Lastly, when you feel ready, connect to the unhealed or unfinished part of you, yourself, that corresponds or matches this person or place that you sent the healing juice to. Feel the energy that you have cultivated during the meditation passing back and forth between you, nourishing you both.

Now have a glass of water and chill out for a bit.

If you'd like me to guide you through this process once or every morning then follow this link here: www.jamiecatto.com/organ-meditation.

How was that? Anything unexpected? You may feel a little raw after the first time, but I hope it has given you an idea or experience of what it feels like to get acquainted with the inner landscape of your body and get used to hanging out there and participating in what your body's wonderful genius is doing on a daily basis. The more we become willing participants in these processes, which means feeling ourselves as fully as we can, the more the body's natural self-mending and maintaining functions can operate successfully.

DON'T TELL ANYONE I SAID 'CHAKRAS'

Now, I know I take the piss out of the new-age side of this stuff and please don't get me wrong, the usual trappings of rainbow dolphins and twinkly unicorns do tend to spoil the practical benefits of these tools for many people who don't want to look woo-woo. As with all genres, however, even heavy metal, there is usually ninety-five per cent which is nonsense and to be avoided, but the five per cent that is juicy is unmissable. The cream of nearly any genre has something wonderful to offer. (OK, maybe not techno).

I have always been a bit suspicious when teachers start talking about chakras, dismissing them as part of the ninety-five per cent nonsense. I don't know why, but perhaps it was because they always seemed to me to represent everything that is smug and earnest about the new-age alternative healer-schmealers. Then, my favourite teacher in the world, Ram Dass, explained them to me in a totally understandable and interesting way, so I am going to risk it here. Ram Dass was the first Westerner to bring Eastern spiritual teachings back from India in a form that made it palatable to the West. He wrote the classic *Be Here Now* at the end of the 1960s. To me he's like half teacher, half stand-up comedian, and always places his own foolishness and fallibility at the centre of his stories and examples. This is an approach that I also keep central in my workshops and events lest we take ourselves too seriously and start proclaiming ourselves reiki masters or something.

The chakras, for those of you who are unfamiliar with the term, are the seven energy points of the body which run from the root, the base chakra, down between your legs, up in seven intervals to the top one, the crown chakra, which is situated at the crown of your head. When you put them all together they make a loop up the back and down the front which maps the main grid of your body's Chi system, and all the other pathways and tributaries of life force that run around your body intersect with this loop.

The lens that Ram Dass describes the chakras through is a bit different, and to me really interesting and something I can relate to. He defines each of the seven chakra points by highlighting them from the point of view of which state of being they represent. Where is your mind thinking from when you operate from each of those centres in your body? So let's go through them as he does:

The First Chakra – also known as the base chakra, this is located up between you legs around the perineum, between your anus and your genitals, and it is primarily concerned with primal survival issues. When our minds are operating from here we are only concerned with food we can eat, air we can breathe, and things which might hurt or kill us. When this area of our lives is threatened it is impossible to think about anything else but survival.

The Second Chakra – this is located just below the belly button and is the creative and sexual chakra. Mostly, when we are operating from here, as we go about our day, all we notice are *fuckable, competitor* and *irrelevant.*

The Third Chakra – this is located at our solar plexus and is also known as the power centre. When we are coming from this area all we can see are people who will help our power in the world, in our careers and missions, and those who might get in our way.

These three centres represent where our species has been operating from for as long as we can remember. But now it starts to get a bit more interesting.

The Fourth Chakra – this one is the heart centre and is where we start seeing everyone more compassionately and less competitively. It is where we feel love and openness and a sense of connection with the other humans around us. It is said that Christ and Buddha came to help us start making a bridge between the third and fourth chakras, and this is where our planet is right now, with many of us working to build that connection to a land where the status-addicted, materialistic forces don't constantly reign.

The Fifth Chakra – this also known as the throat chakra and is concerned with speaking our truth. This is a powerful invitation because it offers the end of manipulation, the end of *working it* or presenting versions of ourselves to get better responses from people. It offers the end of tailoring ourselves into a shape that will be appropriate and palatable for everyone else. It represents authenticity and therefore the portal to true intimacy and connection.

The Sixth Chakra – this one is known as the third eye. It is the part of us that can see it *all*, not just the limited keyhole we usually see the world through. It connects our individual egos with the great Oneness, as from this chakra we are given an aerial view of the overall pattern and where we fit into it, beyond our narrow, individually obsessed perspective.

The Seventh Chakra – this is also called the crown chakra and is the opening or portal for direct contact with the Divine. Christian monks shave that area and Jews cover it. This is the centre where union with the All That Is would be operating from, and I'm not going to pretend to explain what that feels like or looks like. (Let's just say it is probably best for my fragile ego if you don't try and bring me down to your level.)

Using this internal map of seven points to train ourselves to move our attention and breathe up and down our bodies is another good exercise. To practise getting out of our habitually externally focused mind and dropping our awareness down through our whole body is the essence of Full Body Listening. We begin to sense where we are coming from at any given moment or in any situation. Are we always operating from our survival-based first chakra, for example, as a result of lacking any security growing up, or do we feel blocked in our throat chakra, wanting to but always struggling to speak up or speak our truth?

This ability to wander comfortably around the inside of our body is fundamental to catching our minds when they get up to their old tricks of attempting to save us from uncomfortable feelings. The mind is a non-stop, problem-solving machine, and any time we don't feel good it will try to think up something to solve so it can make the uncomfortable feeling go away. This is its automatic response to discomfort, but if you are someone who has pledged to feel all their feelings, not skip them and avoid the edginess, then the mind's preoccupation with solving things that don't necessarily need to be solved can be a distracting nuisance. It is possible to train the mind not to do this and to work on directing our attention *towards* whatever we are feeling, not away from it.

Let me give you an example. The following might be the most liberating, practical and helpful thing I've ever realised.

Sometimes I wake up worrying about money. I wake up in the morning with this gluey, tense feeling in my guts or solar plexus, and immediately my mind starts adding up numbers, working out everything I need to pay for that month and strategising how in the short term and long term I can make this all work out. It is extremely stressful. Later that day someone might ask me how I've been and I might say, 'I woke up worrying about money again this morning . . .'

But wait! That's actually wrong. If I rewind that morning's experience and replay it atom by tiny atom, this is what was really going on: I woke up with this gluey, tense feeling in my guts or solar plexus. It felt really uncomfortable. *Then* my well-meaning yet misguided mind, in order to control and get rid of this yucky feeling in my body, tried to match up the feeling with a story or a concept of something worrying that was going on in my life because it believes, incorrectly, that if my mind can 'solve' that problem or situation then the discomfort will go away.

But this is a trap. It is a decoy that, instead of making the feeling go away, actually makes the feeling get stronger and last longer. The idea of rejecting that feeling, solving it, getting rid of it in this *thinky* way *absolutely does not work*. If anything, it perpetuates it and magnifies it by chewing it over and over.

So, back to me lying in bed. What was really going on?

As we have already established, my body, and yours, is the most genius, self-mending, self-cleaning organism that we know of in the world. Our body is also self-mending and cleaning all our accumulated *emotional* pain and stress in just as sophisticated a way. This is why we wake up, often, with a very uncomfortable tightness or stuckness down our front, somewhere from the throat to the belly. It is not because we have woken up worrying about money, or our health, or any of the mind's versions of what is 'wrong' in our lives. No. It is simply because our genius body/ mind system is doing a well-needed emotional poo. It is offloading some of the accumulation of emotional pain that we all carry, and it cleverly waits until these moments, when we're not so busy thinking, to do its thing.

Getting accustomed to inhabiting our whole body with Full Body Listening allows us to catch the mind when it tries to save us from the uncomfortable task of feeling our feelings and becoming willing participants in what our genius body is doing.

Remember this: *You're almost never worrying about what you think you're worrying about.*

When our minds give us problems to solve, so that once solved we can avoid feeling the constipation, discharging it is the most distracting and useless strategy that sucks us in every time. We lie there in bed, turning that problem over and over, trying to solve it, and this gets in the way of the genius process our body is doing, which is cleverly discharging some accumulated emotional pain or stress.

At these times, if we are skilful we will ignore the mind's version completely and only focus on the physical sensation. If we place our attention on the yucky, tight feeling in the body and gently breathe into it, allowing it, even encouraging it, staying with it in a soft and trusting way, knowing it is part of our body's genius process and not 'something's wrong today', then miraculously it moves, it shifts, it transforms. We need to take the attitude that we are sitting with a child who is consti-pated and feeling insecure. All we need to do is hold its hand, and be there, fully present – nothing more.

TWO PLACES AT ONCE

Many spiritual practices offer up the idea that we each have inside us a Higher Self or a part of us that isn't caught up in the drama and suffering of our human lives. Some call it the Witness or Loving Awareness. Even in our darkest hour we can watch what is going on and discover that inside each of us is a consciousness that isn't sucked in by the whirlwind of feelings yanking us this way and that, a still space which is there along-side the human suffering.

Try this: sit with your eyes closed for four minutes and observe what your crazy mind thinks about all by itself. Don't try and control it or make it calm down, just watch. Very soon you will notice yourself thinking something and maybe that thought will be so seductive that you will forget that you are doing this exercise and follow the thought wherever it goes. But occasionally you will have the experience of noticing yourself thinking, even noticing how compelling the thought is. Thoughts are like that, they whisper, 'Psst, think me, I'm real'. But the point of the exercise is, even if you only manage it once, to notice a thought come and go without getting sucked in. The next question I ask is, if you can notice yourself thinking something then who exactly is watching? Doesn't this prove you are not your thinking mind?

This experience is the key to the door of freedom and the beginning of a life of true creativity.

This practice is the basis of meditation. If you have ever had a meditation teacher who told you to try and still your mind, get your money back. It is impossible to still the mind. The mind is an ever-changing, thinking, up-and-down, in-and-out series of impulses and reactions. You cannot still your mind on purpose. All you can do is observe how *thinky* and busy it is, and if you manage to cultivate the skill of watching each thought come and go without constantly getting carried off unconsciously into whatever story it is telling, whatever problem it is solving, whatever fantasy it is reliving, if you can notice the mind doing its thing and yet remain in the place of the Witness, then the mind, all by itself, may calm down and become still. By not attaching to what it is thinking about but just observing it with equanimity, with appreciation for, instead of resistance to, its busy nature, then there is a chance to become free of its compelling sense of importance. Residing in the place where we are just watching without judgement is freedom. Without learning how to do this we are just a puppet on a string, yanked left and right by whatever new, reactive impulse arises, the victim of whatever the last trigger was that crossed our path.

> If you would like to drop a little deeper into this exploration of what the mind is doing, then repeat the above exercise of watching what your mind thinks about all by itself, and this time, see if you can detect the palette of special effects it is using so successfully to suck you in. Try watching the thoughts with a view to discovering what it is that is so successfully seductive about the mind's techniques. What is in its toolbox of temptation? Does it use feelings or images or threats or hooks? It is worth reflecting on this because without some sort of handle on the mind's machinations we can end up enslaved and unconscious for much of the day. The mind is a wonderful, problem-solving servant but a terrible master.

So, don't believe your mind in the morning when you wake up worrying! It is just your genius doing its work. *Participate* with it, don't resist it. Don't believe the mind's victim story. Breathe into the feeling, let it dissolve and shift – above all *don't think*!

This doesn't only apply to the morning wake-up tension. Our genius body/mind system, or Life itself, is daily sending us difficult and challenging situations and people deliberately to trigger the body into releasing that stuck emotion. I believe that's the very reason adversity exists in our lives. When someone upsets me, if I am skilful, I will feel the familiar volcanic eruption of pain, anger and fear in my chest and instead of fighting that person, I will go straight to the physical place where my body has started discharging accumulated tension and only deal with that person after I have attended to and dissolved what just happened in my body. (Most of the time.)

To be able even to have a chance not to leap straight into battle and control when we are triggered, and to be able to give ourselves an alternative to the solely brain-based way of operating, choosing and navigating our unpredictable lives, and to play a more powerful and participatory role in all the health, communication and inspirational functions our bodies have to offer requires cultivating this Full Body Listening practice. The more embodied someone is, the more trustworthy they feel. The more someone is yapping away, stuck in their head, the more suspicious we are of them. The treasure that is available for us to harvest when we meet Life utilising the full spectrum of sophisticated gifts and skills that come when we prioritise embodiment, with the incredible toolbox of sensations, suddenly gives us the opportunity to live to our creative and intimate potential.

CHAPTER 5

Who Am I and What Am I Doing Here?

Your problem is . . . you're too busy holding on to your unworthiness.

Ram Dass

Have you ever seen that clip on YouTube of the journey the sperm takes to reach the egg? OK, it is a bit banal to say that it's miraculous, but what a trip! Two hundred million sperm get released, more than enough to fertilise every woman in America with just one ejaculation. And only *one* gets to be a human. You! You are a *winner*, job done! If you were in a race with two hundred million other people and you came third, you'd be calling up all your friends, freaking out, going, 'I came third out of two hundred million people!' Well, you didn't come third, you didn't come second, you came first! There's nothing else to achieve, nothing to strive for, no need to do anything that you don't want to do. This life is just the reward, the after-show party, seventy or eighty years of having diverse experiences in a body that can feel emotions and touch and taste and see and hear. Life with a big 'L' is infinite (maybe) but life with a small

'I', this 'me-me-me trip', is finite. You only get a short time being the 'you' that you think you are, and I don't believe it was ever intended to be a make-or-break achievement trip.

So on this journey I feel it is really important to be discerning about which challenges we are going to show up for, and this means examining our relationship with the word 'should'. From an early age our heads are filled with a bunch of incorrect myths and rules about what we 'ought' to do in life. Our choices are so often bound up with our approval addiction, embarking on challenges that we don't really want to do because we think it will make us *a better person* even if the challenge itself doesn't feel attractive. It is almost as if we are coming from the attitude that we can only love and respect ourselves fully at some time in the future when we are *better* at yoga or *better* at getting past our reactivity, or *better* at manifesting ideas of success in our lives.

Is life about achieving anything? Is it about enduring the challenges and looking for things to make us a better person? I feel suspicious about this idea. Sometimes the feeling that we 'should' be doing more or 'should' be evolving faster is really rooted in a deep sense of lack, not a loving sense of wanting to expand into life. It comes from focusing on what we don't have, rather than expanding the bounty we already have. This is a hazardous attitude rooted in scarcity. It's saying that how I am right now is not OK. It's saying that I'm not fully lovable just as I am, and this has far-reaching ramifications on how we treat ourselves and the amount of peace and joy that we think we deserve.

I believe that 'enlightenment' (if it exists) is loving myself exactly as the wounded, freaky creature that I am today. The highest spiritual path that I can attain is to accept myself just as I am, with no agendas or finish lines.

If God (or Life's representative) came into the room right now and said to you that you were never going to evolve another inch, this is as wise as you will ever get, as free as you will ever be, would you still be able to love and respect yourself fully? You have plateaued, and there is no aspect of you that is going to grow any more in this lifetime from this moment on. Can you be a total *yes* to who you are in this moment, as far as you have come, and that's it? Because *enlightenment* is not about getting anywhere in the future or about attaining a level of anything, it is about being totally at peace with where you are right now. Another way to put it is *enlightenment is a realisation not an attainment.* It is the full acceptance and welcome of how things are and the giving up of the struggle and addiction for things to be different. That doesn't mean we shouldn't get excited to grow; it just shouldn't come from a place of scarcity, from a place of believing things shouldn't be as they are. As Shunryū Suzuki-roshi said: 'We are all perfect with room for improvement.' I like that. And the way we can discern whether we're coming from a healthy place or a scarcity-led place is simply to feel inside ourselves and ask, does this feel good? Am I feeling a worry? A sense of scarcity? Or do I feel excited to face a challenge?

There are seven billion people on this planet. Seven billion different versions of how a human can try out being a person. There is no one model that we are all supposed to be adhering to. Yes, it's exciting to show up for challenges, even really hard ones, that feel attractive, but to put ourselves through ordeals and challenges that are only to *make us better* because we think we *should* and can't fully be satisfied with ourselves until we reach a certain point of 'betterness' is more often than not a symptom of lack. Focusing on this lack gives us a constant feeling of *not-enoughness*, which is a bit of a downer to carry around every day.

When we treat ourselves like this we feel disempowered and often find ourselves looking to other people too much, almost in a kind of desperation, to mirror back to us that we *are* OK. (Fuck, I should really listen to this stuff!) We become addicted to external reassurances that we're lovable. We keep pushing to achieve some level of status so that everyone will think we are doing well, because if everyone else thinks we are doing well then that will (very temporarily) anaesthetise us from the painful lack that lives in our bellies.

No amount of status will ever fill that hole if we don't, deep down, feel worthy. Artists like Dave Stewart and Elton John have talked about this at length; it is where the term 'paradise syndrome' comes from. You can play a concert to thousands of adoring fans and they can howl and cheer for you, chant your name, sing along to all your songs, but after the show you are still left with yourself and all your painful, limiting beliefs about yourself. The success and status we achieve in our lives only offers a very temporary fix for the deep-seated sense of lack we feel about ourselves.

I was warned about this very early in life in my first school report: 'He lives his whole life on a stage, but what will happen when the lights go down and the audience go home?' Ouch! They got my number.

While we are obsessing about what other people think of us and judging our worthiness from that perspective, we impose on ourselves an agenda of having to be a certain way for others lest we risk rejection and disapproval. The knock-on effect of this is that we have even more reason to hide much of who we really are and how we really feel from those around us, which limits the connection and intimacy available. It is worth turning this whole perspective on its head. Try allowing others to see *more of you*, especially the parts of yourself you feel are least attractive. Let people see some of the parts of yourself that you find hard to love or that you feel ashamed of – no one else will find them a big deal. They will usually laugh that you felt so ashamed and love you for your wackiness. Try letting others' love lead you back to loving yourself. Let them give you permission to love your so-called unlovable sides.

Whenever we have practised this in a workshop, some people have shamed themselves so unmercifully about 'not being good enough at this' or 'doing that too much' and can take ages being cajoled into disclosing what this huge 'unlovable thing' is. Invariably, when they share what it is, everyone listening looks a bit puzzled and says things like, 'That's *it*? Are you kidding? I do that all the time!', and we all crack up, feeling lighter and a bit sheepish and bemused that we had built up whatever it was into such a phantom.

'What people think' is a vastly overrated issue to concern oneself with, yet it is an often paralysing force, stopping people from daring to live their dream or even speak in public. The people I have coached who are afraid of speaking in public all seem to suffer from the same problem: they are not OK with the idea that anyone might think or see them as a total fool. For me, I already know that me being a total numpty, constantly failing, spilling the wine, saying the wrong thing, is a *given*. And if you are OK with the basic, self-evident truth that 'of course you're a fool, who isn't?' then you are free! Public speaking will be the least of the gifts and relaxation that flows into your life.

You, yes, *you*, are an utter nincompoop. Stop thinking you need to hide that fact and we can all relax and thrive with each other.

We can take this a step further and begin to embrace rather than cower from our critics. The wonderful (now dead) Jesuit priest Anthony de Mello put it brilliantly in his book *Awareness*. He also suggested we stop fighting and disagreeing with people who criticise us. He says that when someone says to him, 'What a stupid thing to say', instead of trying to defend himself he replies, 'You think *that* was stupid? You should have heard what I said yesterday!' Gabrielle Roth is also very clear on the subject. 'Yeah, sometimes I'm a bitch, I'm sometimes everything. *Bitchiness* might be moving through me at a given moment, sure. Why get out of bed every day proclaiming that you're not?'

YOU ARE YOUR KEEPER

My own personal trap, where I look to the external to *make it all OK,* is in my love relationships. As long as I'm the special one, as long as no one else makes you feel how I make you feel, as long as you always choose me, then I can be safe from the demons of lack and abandonment. But annoyingly, when I hand over the job of making me feel good about myself and emotionally safe to another person, I set myself up to live in constant fear of abandonment, because when you stop favouring me and loving me exactly as I want to be loved then my sense of being OK is gone and my whole world falls apart. Depending on the external to make me feel OK about myself is asking for trouble and is very unattractive and draining to one's partner. Instead, I have to cultivate that sense of being OK without constant reassurance from others, precisely because life is so changeable. Other people and situations are never guaranteed to offer a permanent crutch for my insecurity. It sucks, but it is true. Everyone I know will leave or die at some point. Everything I own will someday either belong to someone else or crumble into dust. Life is impermanent and spending all my energy trying to *keep* things the same way will never change that.

Change is the only constant.

Our culture teaches us that once you have gained a certain amount of money and success then everything will be great from then on. We are bombarded by media images of rich people looking happy and so we are brainwashed into thinking that material success will save us from our inner sense of loneliness. Deep down we know it is bullshit but somehow we still cling to the idea and even spend the greater part of each day's energy trying to manifest that reality. Isn't that odd? We know it won't deliver us what we want but we carry on regardless. Isn't that the definition of insanity? To keep doing something we know doesn't work but hope for a different, magical outcome? If anything, achieving those goals can make it worse, because now we have done the thing that promised an end to the loneliness and it didn't work. Now what do we do? This is the point at which a lot of successful people have breakdowns. They have achieved everything society told them would make them feel good but they still feel the same emptiness they've always carried around. What a con!

It is only when we go on an inner journey of self-care that we have any chance of sustainable happiness. In fact, scratch *happiness*. Let's write *contentment* instead, because even the word *happiness* is asking for trouble. As Billy Connolly said in our last 1 Giant

Leap film *What About Me?*: 'I always saw happiness as families throwing beach balls to each other and I was never that guy.'

Happiness has come to imply a life of joy and comfort, free from the darkness and pain, but that's just not realistic. A human life is full of dark and light, pain and pleasure, and pushing away the less comfortable will not only limit the abundant treasure we can harvest from those experiences, it will also give us an unachievable and exhausting burden of trying to make Life's essential nature different from how it really is. However, living a life where we aspire to welcome both the ups and the downs is a more 'wholistic' and realistic approach, to find a comfort in being OK with all the diverse and surprising flavours of existence. Whether we think this is a good idea or not, we don't really have any choice because Life is going to send us a mixture of *what we want* and *what we don't want* whether we like it or not, so there is no point in arguing with reality. The great Indian teacher Krishnamurti said to his students, 'Do you want to know my secret? It is this: I don't mind what happens.'

The key to this contentment is self-care.

HOW WE TREAT OURSELVES

How many times when you *get it wrong* do you give yourself a little electric shock of shaming? 'Ugh! I've done it again!' We can be so violent to ourselves with the habitual pattern of applying the same unkind treatment with which many of our early 'carers' treated us. Not all of them were directly shaming, but passively or actively enforced pressure to 'get it right' and 'obey' was still very much there. Even if we have noticed this and intend to use less aggressive language such as 'I'm so disappointed with myself. I really thought I was past this stuff', it's really no kinder.

There is a great relief in accepting where we are at, with no agenda to be anything else. My life has become so much lighter since I let go of all ambition to grow. Life is going to evolve me whether I like it or not and often send me challenges that I don't want to face. Why push myself into even more endurance tests that don't feel good? This slave-driver mentality has never brought me any joy. Surviving the unexpected ordeals that I had no choice about has taught me many lessons, but forcing myself into situations from some inner sergeant-major belief that I need to work harder, do more, push myself further, feels violent to me, not progressive. It can be a much braver thing not to push myself but accept myself just as I am.

I always say that this path of awareness of all the fallibility and inconsistency of my behaviour as The Man, Jamie is like riding a rodeo horse covered in Vaseline. I'm inevitably going to find myself flat on my arse on the ground a thousand times a day. I have to start finding it funny. If I think it should be different and that I should be doing it better then I am not being realistic. I am exactly as evolved as I am. I am exactly as addicted as I am. I am exactly as un-healable as I am. What is the point in agonising over reality? I can have the intention to grow out of some of my patterns, but as soon as it becomes an addiction to self-flagellation, as soon as I can't be content until I have attained a certain level, I sentence myself to a life of discontent, and no one is the jailer but me.

We have to let go of our accustomed, brow-beating techniques for *making ourselves better*. They are not helping. In fact, if anything, they are sending us in the wrong direction, disempowering and demotivating ourselves with unrealistic, idealised criteria for whether we are worthy of approval or not. It is buried deep in us from the moment we had love meted out to us as children. We only got the unconditional love we needed when we adhered to the adults' versions of who and how we should be. These beliefs, when unchecked, can define how deserving of peace and contentment we think we are. Let's reclaim that authority as of now and dissolve those insidious beliefs that have been ensuring we keep coming up short on the worthiness scale.

Sometimes there is a choice between either going for the experience that seems to offer the fastest evolution, the most fast-track opportunity, or choosing the gentler path, looking after one's fragility. Sometimes we don't allow ourselves the latter choice because we feel we should be braver, or slave-drive ourselves into uncompromising progress, but I say *beware of this*. We are each responsible for looking after this often wounded, vulnerable creature that we are, and for me, that has to come first. We deserve the care that only we can give ourselves.

Bruce Frantzis (page 68) teaches the Taoist principle called the 70% rule, which is that whatever we are doing, whether training physically, mentally or spiritually, we should never use more than seventy per cent effort. This is the best way to ensure steady, sustainable progress without injury or trauma, because if we try to use one hundred per cent effort then we will be likely to overdo it and go beyond our capacity, whereas by starting at seventy per cent we can gently maintain our effort. Pushing ourselves too hard in the name of faster achievement often ends in an injury that can take you out of your practice completely. Ask any Astanga Yoga teacher.

This does not mean that we lower our awareness of our behaviour and just bury our heads in the sand. It is still paramount that we continue to witness ourselves in all our fallible glory. The difference lies in how we react when we catch ourselves acting in a way that is not in alignment with the truth of how we want to be. Are we going to scold ourselves? Are we going to express disappointment with ourselves, or are we going to treat ourselves with total patience and affection? Can we notice all our limitations with no judgement, just loving awareness, and go, 'Aha! There I go again', and smile with affection at our predicament? I look at it as if we all have to become the laughing policeman.

People have different tools and techniques to keep themselves conscious, but, for me, any of them that are the least bit judgemental are violent and off the menu. Affection is the key. Without it, I believe progress is massively limited. Ram Dass talks about how his guru was so playful when he busted him, never judging or serious about it, no expectations for it to be any different by now, but still always there, encouraging, cajoling, and loving him back to consciousness. And even though his guru, the great saint Neem Karoli Baba, is now dead, he still lives in Ram Dass's heart and often speaks to him, laughs at him, reminds him by making his presence felt.

One of my all-time favourite Ram Dass stories is when he was giving a talk somewhere and turned up totally comfortable in his usual guru-like role and attire. He was smiling at the people in the lobby of the venue, being very Ram Dass, and soon the woman who was organising the talk arrived to greet him.

'Hello, Ram Dass!'

'Hello,' he replied in his comfortable, spiritually relaxed way . . . But then, when recounting this story, he said, 'I noticed over the woman's shoulder that the microphone stand they had on the stage wasn't the one we asked for. We always ask for a boom-stand, which has the microphone arm at a horizontal angle, so that if you're sitting cross-legged you don't have to always lean forward to speak into it.' There on the stage was a vertical straight microphone stand, and before he could catch himself, in a totally un-guru-like voice, he pointed. 'What's that?'

'Oh, I'm so sorry,' replied the woman. 'We tried to find you a boom stand but . . .'

'Well, we gave you three weeks' notice,' he heard himself reply, while internally thinking, Ugh! What is this curmudgeonly voice coming out of my head. Who is this I've become suddenly?

'Until,' he said, 'I realised suddenly, just in time, that my guru had come in drag, as a microphone stand, to trigger me!' And he could immediately hear Neem Karoli Baba's voice in his head, laughing at him! 'Ha ha ha, Ram Dass! You're so holy! Do you like the microphone stand?'

Such a beautiful, playful approach!

We are each of us a wise guru in charge of a mental patient.

It is the most accurate description I can come up with for how it is navigating this human life, and although I don't have a guru like Ram Dass's living in my chest, laughing at me so kindly, I have a similar character I have been cultivating who I feel we would all do well to awaken. I carry in my chest a very patient and affectionate psychiatric nurse who is always on call. So when I catch myself failing *again and again*, instead of giving myself a hard time and judging myself with exasperation, as I used to do, now I hear her voice, a very stuff-and-nonsense character, undramatic, saying, 'Are you getting in a bit of a pickle? Do you need a little lie down?', and I place my palm gently on my heart and slowly rub it up and down soothingly while I make the noise you would make to express sympathy to a small child: 'Awww . . . (rubbing the hand gently up and down on the chest) . . . awww, bless . . .'

You can even pinch your cheek gently, dotingly and comfortingly: 'Are you un-healable? Awww . . .'

If we are going to have any chance of setting ourselves free from these repetitive loops of self-sabotaging behaviour, we have to treat ourselves with total love and acceptance, not condemnation. I recommend that we all start to find our failures cute, even adorable. It takes more bravery and discipline to treat ourselves this way than to descend into the usual judging and rejecting we are all so used to. There is no one else but us here to take full responsibility for our self-care. We may have a lover or partner who is very supportive but it is not their responsibility to be our guardian, no matter how naturally caring they are. Once we become adults it is ours and ours alone.

If we want to walk the earth as kings and queens – and by that I don't mean ruling over anyone or being above or better than other people, I mean just walking as ourselves, not manipulating, not *working it*, not controlling or defending or feeling limited in how we give our gifts to the world – we have to be both the king and the butler to the king. We have to be the queen and the lady-in-waiting. We have to embody both roles to look after ourselves efficiently. It is up to the butler to make sure you've slept somewhere comfortable and quiet so you can be rested for the next day. It is up to the lady-in-waiting to make sure the queen has eaten something good before she sets out in the morning. The butler needs to make sure the king is not pestered by too many fools, while the lady-in-waiting steers the queen away from shallow, gossipy environments.

It seems as if all my coaching sessions, mentoring and workshop insights keep leading towards that single concept: self-care.

Am I staying in a situation that doesn't serve me? . . . Self-care

Am I not being met in my relationship? . . . Self-care

Am I giving myself the chance to do what inspires and fulfils me? . . . Self-care

Do I beat myself up with my expectations of how far I should have come by now? . . . Self-care

Am I lonely? . . . Self-care

Am I running to addictions and escapes to avoid my uncomfortable feelings? . . . Self-care

Am I relying on external events and people to feel good inside? . . . Self-care

We've confused self-care with selfishness and abandoned ourselves and our needs. It is time to end the suffering sacrifice. Might it be true that doing what feels good to us is good for everyone?

Patient's Care Document

So, it seems appropriate and useful to take this self-care thing a step further and give ourselves a concrete tool to make sure we are, as the appointed stewards of ourselves, looking after our needs efficiently and diligently. I suggest we all make a self-care document. If we are to be both the patient and the affectionate psychiatric nurse in charge of our own inner mental patient, then there needs to be a file of the patient's notes, history and needs, a care document to make sure we're not vague or uninformed about the job at hand.

I suggest we all structure a document with the following sections and headings:

Profile

1) Warnings: Things to Be Careful of
No one knows your triggers and danger spots better than yourself. What are the things that tend to set you off? What situations would you be well advised to avoid? What kinds of people generally wind you up? Which people already in your life are a drag and need to have their air time with you limited? (And yes, this can, and often should, include your immediate family.)

2) Safeguard Strategies
What are the most dependable tactics to help you get out of a pickle or, even better, to prevent you getting into one in the first place? What helps? What comforts and soothes? What calms you down? What are the kinds of needs and boundaries you need to express when you are about to begin a job, partnership or endeavour? What are the essentials you need to pack in your travel bag? Who are your go-to people in times of crisis?

3) Special Needs to Thrive Best
Where is the best kind of place for you to live? Country? City? What kind of diet suits you? Is there any equipment you need? (I believe every human deserves to have at least a great pair of speakers or headphones. Everyone needs at least one place in their life where they can listen to great sound quality. Music is far too important to scrimp on.) What other entertainments are essential for you?

4) Opportunities for Healing
Wounds and current symptoms/burdens. What is being triggered right now? What are the recent episodes that have hurt or been sticky? What keeps repeating? What are the early patterns that have never quite shifted?

5) Schedule of Care and Programme Activities
What kinds of activities need to be included? What forms of exercise? What fun? Who do you want to hang out with more? How social do you really want to be? Large groups? Small groups? One on one? How do you thrive? What is 'balance' for you? What kinds of days do you feel really great at the end of?

6) Nurse's Skills and Qualities Needed
You are going to be the appointed carer, so what kinds of skills and qualities are you going to need to draw upon? What outside support do you need to bring in? Body workers? Complementary therapies? Treats?

If you want to take it a step further, and I recommend that each of us do, then find a partner and sit down together, preferably having both spent at least forty-five minutes on the above document, and share what you have written. As you go through it point by point and share your care document with your partner, let them interview you for the job of looking after you. Yes, that's right. You need to be interviewed for the job of being your own care worker. Are you up to it? Do you really want to do it? Is there resistance? I suggest the following.

Go into your Full Body Listening mode by bringing your attention to the breath for a couple of minutes.

Sharing your newly written document with the person who's interviewing you for the carer position, go through all the major headings and points and ask the following questions:

1) What would you do and how would you do it? (A plan to deal with each item.)
2) What will the main challenges be that you will have to meet for each item?
3) Where in the body does it live? (Remember the chakras, page 76.)
4) What are the most important ways to inject space in dealing with this item?
5) What support do you need?

A couple of these headings are ambiguous, and I like it that way. If you are the interviewer, make sure you don't impose your insightful wisdom on the carer too much. You are there to support them coming to their own conclusions, not vamp them up with your need to help and be wise. The word 'education' comes from Latin and literally means 'to lead out from within'. Our role is not to add anything but to provide the most likely environment for the person opposite us to discover their own truth.

Whatever we want to achieve in the world, in our missions and projects, whether it be for ourselves or to serve others, unless we are firing on all cylinders, energised and optimised, we are going to vastly limit our chances of success. Self-care, doing what excites us rather than what we ought to do, and treating ourselves with patience and affection are fundamental to achieving the success and fulfilment that is our preferred destiny.

CHAPTER 6

Reframing and Witnessing

Do not fear mistakes. There are none.

Miles Davis

When I was going through my divorce it was messy and scary. I remember getting straight on the plane to London after my ex-wife drew a final line under our marriage and wandering around the streets where I grew up, a bit lost and confused, not knowing what to do or how to begin this next chapter. I felt totally disempowered. At some point I found myself on the tube and one of my favourite, saddest, most heart-breakingly yearning pieces of music came on my iPod. It was 'Passion' by Peter Gabriel. The magnificent soundscape enveloped me as I sat there looking at all the other diverse characters who inhabited my carriage, my gaze drifting from face to face. In my broken state each one of them looked more depressed and alienated than the last. The inconsolable voice of the singer Nusrat Fateh Ali Khan soared. Every aspect of my tragic lostness became truer and truer, and everyone in my vicinity became a validating mirror for how I felt. How was I going to parent my kids now?

Where was I going to live? How could I afford to pay for two homes? What was I going to do now that I was exiled from the family home? My lostness was totally *true* for me in that moment.

But luckily for me, because I always keep my iPod on shuffle, the next tune that came on was 'London Calling' by The Clash, a jubilant, unapologetic piece of rock music that totally transformed my inner landscape within the few bars of the intro. Suddenly my perspective was transforming and I was seeing myself through a completely different lens: 'Who is this hero? Who is this brave maverick? Look at the adversity he is withstanding. Look at his strength, his courage, his lone wolf-like grace!' The tube doors opened and I stepped off, walking tall, electric guitars pumping in my ears, elevating me. I strode down the platform, shoulders back, head held high, and my undeniable heroic majesty was totally *true* in that moment. Wait a minute! A few minutes ago my truth was the total polar opposite of this, what was going on?

I learned a vital lesson that day. We can't control all the crazy shit that's going to happen to us in our lives but we *can* play a part in how we frame it, and *that's* where we can be powerful even in the darkest of times.

This may sound controversial, but I believe in Creation, not arbitrary, accidental bangs. I am not religious and I am not suggesting it was God in six days, but when I observe the beautiful complexity of nature, the exquisite balance of form and function, the structure of a leaf, the breadth of diversity of the creatures on this planet, the combination of tastes and textures and colours of the vegetables and fruits, the existence of consciousness itself with the limitless imagination and compassion and dark and light urges . . . I just do not buy that anyone with any intelligence can say there is more evidence that it was an accidental big bang and not, in some way, possibly, designed. The notion that it was all created by some genius creative force seems like a much more rational and plausible theory to me, given the evidence.

It's a shame to me that religious peddlers have been such murderous dickheads throughout history because you feel like you are lumping yourself in with witch hunters, torturers and right-wing, evangelical Americans if you believe anything but science's totally unsatisfying explanation for the origins of Life, but I have to get past that if I am to be true to my instinct and what seems to be unavoidably self-evident. I don't believe this view excludes Darwin or evolution, rather that that's *how* it was all progressed and developed on Earth, but not *why*. To me, it could still have been designed and then set in motion, and evolution be the system through which it all was set to develop. For me, these views needn't be mutually exclusive. It is the whole masculine/feminine Yin and Yang balance again – that the Creation part emerged out of the feminine, while the masculine made it all happen.

Do we dare to believe that Life's genius has a pattern or an intention? Or is it just too uncool?

WOUNDED IN ALL THE RIGHT PLACES

believe how we frame our reality and whether we are open to seeing that there might be a pattern or not goes a long way to creating how we experience it, and that when something challenging happens it rarely comes without a gift, some sort of illumination. The darkest nights of the soul have also trained us in our most vital, emotional survival abilities. So, do we frame what happened as a tragedy or as a valuable training? It depends where we want to focus. When something challenging happens to me, I can either frame it as a negative where I am the victim of whatever just happened or, if I shift my lens of perception, I can see it as a possible illumination or a valuable lesson. Challenges rarely come without rewards when we take the second approach. There's always some gold in them hills if we focus our telescope to a more open and curious setting.

In astrology (it's OK, I'm not hanging any crystal dolphins on your head) they have an archetype called Chiron, the Wounded Healer, which represents this concept perfectly. The very things we have survived are huge signposts to the essential gifts we are going to bring to the world. It might not feel like it at the time, of course, but anyone who has been through some heavy shit in their lives would rarely, after the event, exchange that experience for anything. It may have yielded wisdom and courage and the ability to be generous. Think of some of the most challenging experiences of your life. Now that they are over, would you cancel them out? I doubt it. Think of what they gave you, how they moulded and educated you. Within those answers you'll discover clues to the gifts you have to offer in your projects and missions.

The Chiron Game

Here's a game to harvest that reframing side of your nature, and it is a great way to experiment with different aspects of your newly acquired Full Body Listening. OK, here goes . . .

Put on some gentle music, close your eyes, and spend four or five minutes feeling where in your body the sensations begin

---

to be felt, just being with it, not needing to analyse or grasp. Just allow the feeling to be wherever it is and clock it.

Sit comfortably with a vaguely straight spine and turn on your Full Body Listening. Feel the thinky mind surrender a little to the softer, listening field. Go empty and feel yourself from crown to toes as a sophisticated receiving device. No need to rush this. Listen to your breath for a little, feel your whole body. Then, when you feel settled and open, I want you to tune into the time or times in your life where you had to endure the heaviest dark nights of the soul. I am talking about those times when there was no one there to support you, or you couldn't connect to the help that was being offered. Those times when you were barely hanging on by a thread and had to make it until dawn, alone and scared.

When you feel more connected and settled into that realm in yourself, ask yourself the following questions. Allow a little time for each question to percolate and feel any resistance to answering fully, don't rush. See how total you can be in your responses:

1) What have been the most challenging things about these experiences?
2) What skills or qualities have I needed to develop to overcome or cope with those experiences?
3) What am I better at, or more sensitive to, through all this?
4) What have I been being trained in here?

When you have allowed these questions to lead you wherever they will, consider them from both the fleshy human and the observing witness's perspectives. We have felt into the memories of what it was like, but now, from just the observing presence's viewpoint, the one in you that is open to how even the hardest periods might be part of Life's genius doing something benev-olent and illuminating, ask the golden question:

If I had set this up as a superhero, survival-training exercise and then forgotten about it, what special super powers was I being trained in? What valuable, even essential gifts do I now have?

Just as my own journey with panic attacks prepared me for a life of supporting others who suffer from similar conditions, I invite you to include the harvest of what you have survived in your life in your creations, projects and missions. On the plane where life is one long curriculum, let's reap the benefits of what we've been through and reframe our sad stories as the advanced training and skill-gathering missions that they are.

Take a short break, maybe dance, get the body moving, and when you're ready, settle down for the second part of the game.

*

We have come up with some good data so far, but have still been at least partly in the more cerebral – masculine or Yang – side of our minds. For me, the really great unexpected stuff has more chance of arising when we drop deeper into the intuitive – feminine or Yin – space which bypasses the thinking, calculating mind. Try this:

Connect to the one in you who endured and survived those times, the character who was there, who always lives in you, the survivor. I want you to tune into that character who lives in you now.

We are going to invite that character in, which is not something we are accustomed to doing. That character usually only appears in a crisis, and our painful and traumatised associations with it don't inspire the attraction to invite them in deliberately. But just as an experiment, invite this surviving character to come a little closer, to be welcome here with us right now.

There are numerous techniques for meeting up with your inner characters and making a connection. Some say, 'You are getting into a lift . . . the doors close . . . you go down floor after floor . . . the doors open . . . you are in a garden with a stone bench . . .' and if that helps you ease into it then go for it, but all you really need to do is feel that character, feel the desire to welcome them in, bring them closer, and in your Full Body Listening state allow that sense of feeling them near to happen. If you are more visual, you may see the character in your mind's eye come and sit down next to you, or if you are more sensory you may just feel the presence of the character. Don't worry about exactly how it manifests itself; whatever way this character arrives that feels natural to you is the right way for you to do it.

When you feel ready, we are going to interview that character by asking questions and listening deeply for the answers, and the way we do this is by writing the questions with our usual writing hand, and then once the question has been asked (written) we are going to transfer the pen to our unusual writing hand and listen and listen and empty and empty, and whatever answer we hear coming back in our inner ear, we simply transcribe in our wonky, wrong handwriting.

So when you feel your own Chiron superhero is with you, put the pen in your usual writing hand and start a conversation. The first thing to express (by writing) is:

Thank you so much for going through so much to earn us these super powers.

This might be the first time we have offered this character the gratitude and appreciation it deserves, and even though that is not a question, when you transfer the pen into your unusual writing hand and empty and empty and listen and listen, before very long, you will hear a response. All you have to do is listen and transcribe what comes. Then when you feel the response is complete and you have given it plenty of space, transfer the pen back into your usual writing hand, and ask:

What support do you need to express your super powers and creative and healing force in the world?

Then once again, transfer the pen back into your unusual writing hand and empty and empty and listen and listen, and whether it takes a few seconds or a couple of minutes, when you hear the response, simply transcribe it. When you feel the response is complete and you have given it plenty of space, transfer the pen back into your usual writing hand, and ask: How and where can I give these gifts to myself and others?

And once again, transfer the pen back into your unusual writing hand and empty and empty and listen and listen, and transcribe the answer that comes, and then again, when you feel the response is complete and you have given it plenty of space, transfer the pen back into your usual writing hand, and ask:

How shall I call on you?

With Batman, they shine a bat shape up onto the clouds. Dorothy has to click her ruby-red slippers together and say 'There's no place like home'. How does your superhero like to be summoned?

If you feel like a bit of fun, either alone or with your pals, come up with a superhero name for your inner survivor.

This reframing and allowing the idea of Life's genius being benevolent is a cornerstone of harvesting the unexpected and often challenging episodes we are all living through. Yes, we can go to fortune tellers and healers, pull tarot cards, journey with shamans or even have some reiki, but all the most potent information is to be sourced directly from ourselves, by giving ourselves enough space and stillness to listen and not always farm out the work we need done to others. It is good to get support, but not instead of trusting our own abilities to know what is real and essential for us. No matter how sensitive someone else is, they will always get a second-hand version of what's inside you.

'It takes immense discipline to be a free spirit.'

I love this line by Gabrielle Roth . . . because it is the easiest thing in the world to gravitate towards the suffering and victim-centred version of events. It is what everyone around us has been doing for their whole lives. It takes a conscious choice not to succumb to that low, disempowered road.

This doesn't mean we focus on the gifts *instead of* feeling the soreness of what is going on. Far from it. Many people have tried to use these practices of reframing as a way out of feeling the human pain and chaos of these challenges. In spiritual circles it is called *running upstairs* or *spiritual bypassing*. As a way to try and avoid feeling the human waves of discomfort, there are some who would like to use the more accepting and optimistic witness's version as an escape. This often comes with proclamations that 'It's all meant to be!' But this practice is not to escape but to go deeper, and to keep the full, visceral human experience while also giving it the context and added harvest of the gifts it brings. It is a way of experiencing both at once, the human going *Ouch that fucking hurts*, while the witness is compassionately collecting the bounty. Once again, this is how we become powerful in our lives, not the victim of suffering nor the disembodied, self-abandoning pain-avoider looking only on the bright side. An illuminating human life is experienced with a foot in each camp, living both upstairs and downstairs at the same time, both on the stage and in the audience, resisting the drama and enjoying the show.

When we consider that the unexpected and often abrupt scene changes of our lives might be benevolent, we join the lineage of intrepid discoverers who have preceded us. Big band leader Glenn Miller was searching for his musical 'sound' for years, trying out different arrangements, never quite finding the 'thing' he was searching for, until one day a bunch of his musicians were unable to get to the concert they were playing that night and he had to, as an emergency measure, give all the melodies to the bass brass instruments. This was a very unusual thing to do, as traditionally it is the higher sounds that hold the lead melodies and the bass sounds hold down the rhythm. He didn't have a choice on this occasion and so the clarinet and tenor saxophones held the melodies while the other saxophones played complementary harmonies, and the unique and world-famous Glen Miller Big Band sound was born.

Charles Goodyear spent years trying to find a way to make rubber resistant to heat and cold. After a number of failed attempts he finally stumbled across a mixture that worked. Before turning out the lights one evening he accidentally spilled some rubber, sulphur and lead onto a stove, resulting in a mixture that charred and hardened but could still be used.

Leaving space for failure or reframing what our idea of 'failure' is opens up a treasure trove of possibilities. When Thomas Edison invented the lightbulb, his nay-sayers pointed to the pile of thousands of non-functioning prototypes and said, 'But look at all those failures!' Edison coolly replied that those weren't failures, they were thousands of ways of finding the right way to do it. The guy that invented the X-ray camera was said to have been trying to invent a way to photograph fairies! This is why I always suggest that in our creative projects and missions, we try to embody the paradox of having a super-clear vision to head towards, but to make sure it is a flexible vision, because Life's genius has a knack of turning left suddenly and creating something even better than we first intended. We have to be flexible and open to allow that possibility to unfold. As my favourite extraterrestrial Bashar says, we need to redefine our concept of a roadblock: 'Roadblock: an arrow pointing in an unexpected direction I didn't realise I needed to go in.'

This idea of letting Life live us instead of imposing our own plans upon life includes the admission that, although we think we know best and are clear with what we want, the viewpoint from which we are perceiving our world is very limited. We are looking out through a letterbox version of *reality*. We can't see a very broad spectrum, not even as far as infrared or ultraviolet. We can't hear a particularly wide range of sound either, for example the high frequencies that dogs can pick up or very far into the lower decibels. Of course, we have to make do with what we've been given, but including an acknowledgement that there might be all kinds of forces at work which we can't perceive is not such an implausible leap of faith.

Dancers and surfers have an advantage here because those are two activities where you have to surrender in order to succeed. We dance most enjoyably and freely when we let the music move us, yet it can feel very vulnerable to do this as no one wants to look ridiculous. Hence William W. Purkey's famous adage:

You've gotta dance like there's nobody watching,
Love like you'll never be hurt,
Sing like there's nobody listening,
And live like it's heaven on earth.

Surrender! Life has its own genius that often knows better. To have the courage to live life this freely means letting go of our obsession with never risking failure or looking like a fool. It means facing adversity in a less paranoid fashion. When an unexpected left-turn jolts us out of our comfort zone, instead of trying to wrestle it back, the trust in Life asks the question: 'What might I be trying to show myself?' You can call it pronoia: the sneaking suspicion that that man across the street who is going into that building is doing something that is going to make my life better.

What if not getting what we want is as interesting and useful as getting what we want?

What if we gave permission to ourselves to let go of our belief that we are unworthy?

What if we began to walk into the shadows to meet our demons, play with our demons, and be our honest, true, vulnerable selves rather than the edited version we grew up believing we ought to be?

CHAPTER 7

Playing with our Demons

What would the earth look like if all the shadows disappeared?

Mikhail Bulgakov

In the spirit of reframing our more challenging experiences I feel it is useful to re-examine the role of the ego and question what a bad reputation it tends to get. We have been playing with the idea that an efficient and empowered life has to be lived in two places at once. We are the human ego personality who's here having a 'me-me-me trip', totally invested in the perspective that 'I am an individual', separate from all the other individuals, needing to compete and compare myself with the other egos who are buzzing around, and totally (usually) sucked into the drama on the stage. And at the same time our ego lives in parallel with the less volatile *witnessing* part of ourselves, which by the same metaphor is in the audience just watching, not getting caught up in the drama, not judging and condemning ourselves for our constant imperfections and mistakes but maintaining a degree of equanimity while all the ego-based drama is unfolding.

Because, in our modern culture, the balance between these two parts of our awareness has fallen into such radical imbalance, with hardly anyone cultivating the witness and instead mostly concerning themselves with satisfying the demands and terrors of the ego-based part of our consciousness, it makes sense that spiritual and self-development systems make it central to their game plan to try and bring the two back into balance. However, some among these practitioners and students have got it into their heads that they are meant to eradicate the ego and only live in the witness space. The word 'ego' strikes terror into them as they have been working so hard, sweating away in meditation halls, to amputate this nasty, unspiritual ego thing so that their pure light of divinity can shine through. In fact, in most new-age circles that I have come across, the word 'ego' doesn't even mean 'ego', it means 'asshole', and it is a convenient, un-self-betraying way to criticise someone without appearing to be too judgemental.

Someone comes into the yoga studio looking buff and pleased with themselves, drops into a perfect series of asanas, and a faux-spiritual yogi over the other side of the hall nudges his friend, nods in the direction of the offender and they roll their eyes, muttering the condemning verdict: 'ego'. He doesn't mean 'ego', he means 'wanker'. These 'ego amputators' are so afraid of failing in the assumed-to-be most important category of being spiritual, being 'beyond ego', that seeing someone being unapologetic in their presence stirs up a volcano of judgemental unkindness.

As we have been born on earth to have an experience of being an individual, it is impossible to navigate this body and mind around the planet *without* an ego. It is like the little man in the video game that you are operating from outside the screen with your joystick and buttons. How can you play the video game without the little fella running around, jumping and being subject to all the missiles that the game throws at it? You can't. To try and exist in a human body without an ego isn't going to work. Unless there is an 'I' to witness and to forgive and to love unconditionally, no matter how repetitively he fails, there can be no game and this wonderfully diverse theme park of limitations, with all its angelic and diabolic possibilities, cannot be experienced. The Earthworld theme park would have to shut down without all the little egos running around.

That is not to say that we let the egos run the show. They do need to be kept in check, and balanced by the observing presence of the patient witness, and yes, God help us if they think they are the only one here. A life which is totally consumed with ego concerns is a nightmare of reactivity and anxiety. But just because the ego needs to be brought back into balance does not mean that it is bad, shallow or unenlightened to have one. In fact, once you have the ability to enjoy the ego within its context, you can really start enjoying this planet and lead a guilt-free life of touches, tastes, sounds, sights and feelings.

I was once teaching a creativity workshop, a project-building master class, much of which I have written about in chapter 10, 'Unleashing the Genius', and we were playing a game where we totally let the ego off its leash, let it blow itself totally out of all proportion, to dissolve all limitations of bigness and success we might have been carrying. The ceiling of our success and pleasure is rarely externally enforced. No matter what luck and opportunities our lives bring us, if we have a lack of permission around how much success it is OK to enjoy, those limiting beliefs will define the ceiling of success that we can manifest.

It is the same with intimacy. When you are making love, no matter how skilful your partner is in his soulful and erogenous zone-arousing techniques, even if you are in bed with Billy 'Tantric Fingers' McGinty, your permission around your own pleasure will be the ultimate limitation of how much ecstasy you will be able to feel. So, in the workshops we play some games where we are invited to explore going totally balls (or ovaries) outwith our ego-trips. We play at highlighting all the places where we lack permission to express our unique genius. It blasts away the cobwebs where we have been hiding our power and shines a spotlight on where we are playing small in order not to be rejected by those who are stirred up around powerful people.

When it came time to play the game, as usual, I explained the rules to the group, and as usual you could immediately see the whites of the eyes of all those present who considered themselves 'spiritual'. I remember one guy who was mortally offended by what I was suggesting he do. He came up to me to explain why he refused to take part in the game. 'It's just ego, ego, ego!' he said. 'I've meditated for twenty years to be free of this stuff! I don't see any benefit in regressing back to that unevolved state again!' I looked at him quizzically and asked, 'Are you so much of an egomaniac that you can't even pretend to have a big ego – even in a game?'

He froze. His eyes went moist. A soft smile of surrender spread over his tense face and before very long he was the craziest playmate in the group. It was such a release to see him cavorting and posturing around after the long-suppressed permission had kept him and his creative expression in a straitjacket. You see, to be free of something is not the same as getting rid of it. To be free means we are neither grasping nor rejecting things. We are neither clinging nor pushing away. While we are pushing things away they still have us, we are still trapped by them. How many rebels have you met who are reacting against conformity rather than who are truly free? It is a subtler prison, but no less confining. Trying to amputate your ego is a kind of self-castration in the name of spiritual attainment. If any teachers take that kind of a line with you, call me.

The ego, when celebrated, is a big part of how we bring our unique flavour to the world because it is the home of all our preferences. Our individual tastes and turn-ons that we want to generously share with the other humans are rooted in the individuated ego. I'm a staunch advocate of fully enjoying our egos without letting them think they are totally running the show. So we need some tools to strike that balance where we are not limply excluding ourselves from all the fun on offer on this planet but neither are we unconsciously bouncing back and forth between all our ego-driven attractions and repulsions. Much of the sabotaging side of our out-of-balance ego behaviour is supported by how amazingly sophisticated the little sucker has become. It slips in insidiously and because we haven't noticed that it has taken the driving seat, it is impossible to be conscious and discerning about it.

That is why many of the games that we play are about tying bells to our ego-characters' ankles so you hear them coming a mile off and don't get seduced by their compelling urges.

THE INNER CRITIC GAME

One of the first games I like to play to get right into the heart of one of our most dominant and destructive demons is the Inner Critic Game. I start with the 'inner critic' because it is one of the most universal, insidious voices we carry around with us, that undermining, unpleasant voice that crops up from time to time in our heads, ready to remind us how rubbish we are, how hopeless it all is, and how we have wasted our lives. What a cheery character! On one level, we allow the Inner Critic its voice so that we will keep our ego in check and never get too big for our boots, but is it really helping? I doubt it. Is the habit of constantly, unconsciously shaming ourselves keeping us motivated? I don't think so. Yet we allow this toxic dominator to hold court in our brains while we struggle on, doing our best to dodge its mean whiplashes or worse, meekly submitting to them.

I am not interested at this point in getting into the psychotherapeutic techniques of examining where it came from, which parent or carer or combination of their voices we accidentally internalised when we were too immature to screen out the negative feedback that we were subjected to as we grew up. It can certainly be useful to go down those roads, but I have found meeting the characters in the present moment to be even more fruitful. It is *now* that they are presenting their symptoms and wreaking havoc in our brow-beaten minds, so I find it more entertaining and useful to play with them in the here and now.

This is a game we play in three stages, ideally with a few friends but you can also play it alone, so let's jump straight into it.

First, as we did in the Chiron superhero game, we are going to welcome in the Inner Critic, and instead of resisting and trying to push it away, we are going to invite it closer and let it have its say. The way that we do this is to give it the pen and let it say all the mean, undermining stuff that it wants to while we offer it our services as secretary, simply transcribing everything it spews out.

So as before, we grab a pen and paper and sit comfortably, spine vaguely straight, and return to our breath. We notice we are breathing in and we notice we are breathing out, not doing anything clever with the breath, just noticing and returning to ourselves in a settled, rooted way before we commence.

Next, we consciously turn on our Full Body Listening, which we are getting pretty good at by now, and prepare to welcome in our Inner Critic in much the same way as we invited our Chiron to come and sit down next to us. Whatever feels like the natural way to do this is the right way for you, whether it is a character you can see visually in your mind's eye or more of a sensory connection to it, the Inner Critic has an easily discernible flavour and when we spend a few minutes inviting it closer you will soon enough feel it is time to hand over the pen.

This is where our Full Body Listening is most important. We are not thinking up something for the Inner Critic to say, we are softening back into the listening field and going empty, patiently waiting for the Inner Critic to start sharing with us all the undermining, negative opinions and warnings it has for us, so that we can transcribe it, let it use our pen and hand to get it all down onto the page. This doesn't need to be hurried; it can take as long as a few minutes to get started, as we might not be accustomed to surrendering in this way. When the Inner Critic starts telling you how useless you are, and often, how pointless this exercise is, just write it down without editing or judgement. Some emotions might bubble up while you are writing. Stay with them, allow them, trust that the body/mind genius might be using this opportunity to redistribute some old stuck emotional Chi. It may feel a little uncomfortable, but do your best to allow yourself to be a willing participant in all the feelings and become fascinated by any sensations that are moving in the body, both physical and emotional. You might not feel any discomfort at all; in fact, you might find the shit this Critic comes out with hilarious now that you have taken a step back from it. Either way, totally surrender to the flow of words and for about fifteen minutes just fill the page with whatever your uniquely judgemental Inner Critic has to offer today.

When you are done, move your body around, maybe put on some music and have a dance, drink some water and come back to yourself. If you need a break, listen to that need. Make sure you are intimate and self-caring enough with yourself throughout the exercise so that you don't force yourself through anything that doesn't feel OK. Don't trample your own boundaries. If the feelings which arise are too much to deal with right now, listen to that. There is no parent here whose job it is to notice how you are feeling and what you need, so be your own butler or lady-in-waiting, be your own parent, and don't push yourself further than feels OK for you. There are no prizes for über-boldness in these games. Your self-care is paramount and you have to have your Full Body Listening on at all times so that you can constantly monitor how this feels.

*

OK, let's move on to the second stage.

Get a new piece of paper and write down the following list:

1) Over-exuberant porn star in the middle of a scene.
2) Spoiled, whining child.
3) Enthusiastic, cheesy game-show host.
4) Drunk or stoned person.
5) Fascist dictator.
6) Your mother

Now gather in your group of friends, or if playing by yourself, stand in the middle of the room, or if you dare, in front of a mirror, with your newly written Inner Critic script and find a dice (or dice app). When it is your turn, roll the dice, and whatever number you throw, perform your Inner Critic script in the exaggerated voice of the number that you threw. For instance, if you throw a two, return to your group and perform everything you wrote when you were channelling your Inner Critic in the voice of a spoiled, whining child. I recommend that you have at least two goes each trying out different character voices, and I always suggest that everyone has at least one go at throwing a number three. For some reason it seems to be the most powerful medicine for popping the Critic's gravitas bubble and removing any chance of your taking that voice to heart ever again.

One more thing, if you throw a number one then you are allowed to use one of the other members of your group as a prop (as long as it's consensual).

Have fun with it and embrace the foolishness. Without playfulness it's impossible for wisdom to thrive.

*

Are we ready for the third and final stage? We have now covered the liberation side of the game by tying a good few bells to the ankle of your once insidiously crafty demon. Now it is time to harvest its gifts.

Earlier in the book we looked at how our unconscious,

negative beliefs can cause huge amounts of painful over-reactivity when events don't unfold as we would wish. Beliefs about what we deserve, what we can handle, about what is inevitably going to happen to us, and how we are powerless. Lists of unconscious beliefs that we spend our lives trying to protect ourselves from and that run in self-sabotaging loops, upsetting us and often inducing us to make some terrible choices.

This script that your Inner Critic has just downloaded for you offers a list of many of the disempowering, negative beliefs you are running just below the surface of your everyday actions and thinking. I want to diligently dissolve these limiting ideas one by one, and so I am grateful that my Inner Critic performs this vital function of giving me a vivid menu of my negative beliefs in list form.

So when it says 'You are lazy' I know that somewhere deep down, no matter how much work I am doing, I have internalised a belief from long ago, probably from a teacher at school, that I am not working hard enough and that I am lazy. Once I realise that I've got this old, incorrect belief knocking about in my unconscious, bringing me down with a negative view of myself and leaving me feeling inadequate no matter how hard I am striving, I have the chance to decide not to believe it any more. Once I bring my awareness to it, it is no longer a habit and becomes a choice.

The way to harvest the script that you just played with is to go through it line by line and start a new list, turning each of the statements in it into an 'I' statement. So, for instance, if it says 'You are lazy' then you write 'I am lazy' on your new list. If it says 'No one likes you', then you write 'No one likes me' on the new list. Once you have gone through the whole script you will have an unmissable menu of all the ways you are undermining yourself. This is a juicy tool for transformation. It is time to question all these beliefs, which are really incorrect conclusions you drew as a child from the negative feedback you received from careless parents, teachers and peers.

Once you have that list of statements, the first thing is to add a question mark at the end of each one, and then read it again. Do not think about it too much, just turn it into a question, consider it, and reflect for a few moments on the veracity of the idea.

At this point Byron Katie would ask her four questions, and asking each of them for every item on your list is an illuminating and often liberating journey:

1) Is it true?
2) Can you absolutely know that it is true?
3) How do you react, what happens, when you believe that thought?
4) Who would you be without the thought?

Having asked the four questions, Katie then proceeds to do what she calls a 'turn-around' for each of the beliefs. Try reversing the negative statement into a positive one and see what resistance arises in your body. It is great fodder for tracking and dissolving these chains, a real commitment of liberation.

'I am lazy' becomes 'I am hard-working'.

'No one likes me' becomes 'Everyone likes me'.

'I'm weak' becomes 'I'm strong'.

*

Katie is definitely the queen of busting these paralysing beliefs and supporting thousands of people in transforming their disempowerment though unvarnished self-enquiry.

For each of the beliefs on your list, it is well worth asking yourself where you might have picked it up. Was it a parent or another family member who first gave you that idea about yourself or was it one of your teachers or classmates? When might it have happened and, most especially, where in your body does it get uncomfortable when you stir up the feelings associated with this belief?

Feel the difference in your body as you play with these statements and allow the sensations to lead you out of your restrictive mindset. You will notice that pretty much every point on the list is something someone gave you that was never yours, and as Bashar says: 'Picking up other people's baggage is called stealing. Put it down.'

We are here to dissolve the lattice of these unconscious beliefs that hold all limitation in place. Even our mean, undermining Inner Critic, when treated skilfully, has his uses when you harvest his verbosity and show him who is the boss. He will lead you straight to his hideout where he keeps all the ammunition you use against yourself and which, with the help of your Full Body Listening and self-care, you can use to reframe all those negative beliefs and begin to let go of all that old, accumulated baggage.

DYSFUNCTION AND THE CINDERELLA GAME

The key to the Transforming Shadows method I use in my workshops is to stop running scared from the posturing and punking of our demons, and instead whip their little asses and begin to turn them into employees, even allies.

This next game addresses where these pesky little critters might have come from in the first place. Rather than just write them off as random symptoms of early wounding, I like to allow in the idea that these dysfunctionally behaving characters might also be integral messengers from Life's genius. Before I go deeper into that notion, for the next game I'd like you to choose one of your most repetitive, dysfunctional patterns or 'characters' who live in you, seemingly immune to all healing and 'working on it'. Choose a self-sabotaging behaviour that no matter how long you have been trying to shift, doesn't seem to change very much. 'Whenever (this happens) . . . I always (react like this) . . .'

For example, maybe you automatically get confrontational and start a fight every time you feel vulnerable, or perhaps, like me, you find it hard not to collapse into disempowerment and panic whenever you feel jealous. It's almost as if we become a totally different person in those moments, as if a character who has been lying dormant in our heads suddenly awakens and jumps into the driving seat.

When these characters or reactions are triggered and start leaping in with their troublesome agendas, it is so unsettling and often painful that our instant reaction is to try and suppress, reject and hide them away. Although on the surface this makes perfect sense, in that we do not want these 'ugly' sides of ourselves to come into plain view, that pushing-away attitude means we miss out on the more potent invitation that is being offered. Once again, I am an advocate of treating the situation as if it might be an opportunity, rather than falling straight into the controlling, victim-led habit of pushing away any or all of the parts of ourselves we have come to label as wrong or inappropriate.

Have you chosen one yet?

The chances are, if this is one of your regular, more ingrained characters, you already know its flavour pretty well and have been trying to hide it away for a very long time. This is largely why it has never shifted. The way you are currently framing it, it is a total drag when it crops up again and again. I want you to reacquaint yourself with it and question how it came to be here in the first place. What I have discovered is that these characters who live in us, even the seemingly destructive ones, were actually created by us as helpers or supporters at a time in our lives when we didn't believe we could cope with whatever was going on and felt we needed the support of a character like this to survive. They didn't just magically appear as fallout from our traumas and difficulties. We created them as a coping strategy.

For example, a man who attended a workshop told us about being the youngest of six siblings, and that when he was a kid sitting at the dinner table he needed to shout the loudest to be heard and elbow his way to getting enough food on his plate in a bit of a grabby way. This survival strategy made sense at the time, but now that he was thirty-six years old it was no longer working for him. What was once a vital way to get what he needed as the youngest of six was now a self-sabotaging part of his life, so that others were labelling him antisocial and deliberately not inviting him to things. Yet the character in him that was unconsciously behaving in this way was totally well-meaning – it was given his instructions long ago and no one ever told him to stop.

These characters – the good girl, the clown, the peacemaker, the defender – all think they are helping, and it is confusing, and if anything a little disheartening, to be constantly rejected and dismissed when they appear. In this context, our treatment of our less attractive characters is unjust and needs redressing.

So, if you would like to transform the character you have chosen for this game, let's start by putting on a gentle bit of music, sitting comfortably, turning on our Full Body Listening and, as before, invite them in.

First off, lean into the quality of feeling that arises in you when this character is triggered. By now you might find that you become quickly aware of a physical sensation somewhere in your body. Your breath might be affected, you may feel some emotion.

Stay with it, and place the palm of your hand on the area of your body where the feelings are waking up. When you feel closer to the flavour of this issue or character, wonder very gently about when in your earlier life you might have needed its support. What was going on back then that you needed a being with these qualities to be with you so that you could cope with whatever was going on. When might you have brought it into being and to do what job for you? Was it there to protect you? Was it there to help you escape or hide? Was it there to communicate with challenging parents or carers or bullies who you felt disempowered around? Was it created to stand up for you when you felt overcome? What else might it have been? Without rushing or getting over-analytical, relax back into the feeling and let the answer unfold: When might I have created this character and to do what job or jobs for me? How did it serve me to create this character? What was going on?

*

The next stage can be done alone, with a partner or with a small group of good listeners. First, delve a little deeper into the process and articulate what job you think you created your presently dysfunctional character for. Try and focus more on how things felt for you at that time more than recounting all the details of every instance you remember. It isn't wrong to describe what was happening with specifics but it is also very easy to get distracted and lost in the stories of what happened, and although it is helpful to illustrate what your life was like around that time, how it felt for you usually yields the best results when imagining what role you created this character to play for you.

If you are recounting to others, the listeners can feed back and ask questions for clarity, but as before in the Chiron game, their job is to let you come to your own realisations, not project their own opinions and ideas on to you. I mention this a lot because we are so used to helping in a more masculine way, which suggests things and comes up with reasons for each other, sometimes from an agenda of solving and getting to a finish line rather than holding space patiently with no need for it to go anywhere specific. Sometimes it can be hard, as a listener, to let people stay in discomfort or lack of clarity, so trained are we to find solutions for things and tie them up and get past them that we hurry the journey of discovery. It takes steadfastness and patience to be a Full Body Listener in this context, so I invite you to be extra clear about it. It reminds me of a line from a poem called 'The Invitation' by Oriah Mountain Dreamer: 'I want to know if you can sit with pain, mine or your own, without moving to hide it or fade it or fix it.'

Once you feel you have covered the question of what was going on in your life back then, that meant you needed to create this character, and what supportive or protective jobs you created this character to do, the next stage is to make a list of all this character's skills. Yes, right now it is most likely using its skills in negative, self-sabotaging ways, but it still does have skills. That dominating, grabby youngest-of-six-siblings is great at getting enough for himself even though he is doing it in a way which is antisocial at the moment. He is great at being heard, at surviving, and even though he is using his skills in a way that needs to be transformed, the skills are still there; they just need to be retuned.

In my own life, when I consider the needy, abandonment-phobic guy who lives in me, he definitely has skills, too. For example, he has supremely refined CCTV skills. He can detect the Skype noise or the Facebook message noise from three rooms away. He can sense when someone's affection or attention is leaving him. He is so paranoid about being left that he has developed a hyper-sensitive radar for all this stuff. Usually what he does with that information is to make me even more paranoid, which can often result in my making a fuss about something that pushes my partner away instead of vulnerably sharing my fears and asking for support. Yet those skills could be used to support me in my life in a much more conscious and healthy way if I dare to enter a new dialogue with my character and let go of the perceived control he gives me. To embrace his powers of intuition without lurching into control-freak mode.

Make a list of all your character's skills, even ones you may judge as unhealthy or dark. They are all transformable. Don't hold back and, if you are with a partner or a group, use their help, as they have more distance and less shame around this story than you and will likely suggest abilities that you hadn't thought of. Get them all down on a piece of paper so you can look at them there with new, unprejudiced eyes.

*

For the last stage, it is time once again to leave the masculine side of our nature, which has had a good run at the conceptual, penetrative side of this enquiry, and melt back into the feminine, listening field. We are going to enter a new dialogue with this character by conducting an interview, asking our questions by writing to the character with our usual writing hand and emptying and listening for the answers which we then transcribe, having transferred our pen to our unusual writing hand. We don't want to banish this character, and we couldn't even if we tried. These parts of us, once created, can't be uncreated, so instead of trying to get rid of them, which is both impossible and ungrateful, how about employing them with a new job? All it has ever wanted to do was help and support but we have rejected it and tried to hide it away, while it has, to its own best knowledge, been working tirelessly to do the job we asked of it. That is why I call this game the Cinderella Game, because we never acknowledge the character's well-meaning hard work and certainly never let it come to the ball. It has to stay hidden away in the basement, out of sight.

As before, use whatever gentle pathway to inviting in this character that feels natural to you. I won't describe the whole process in detail again here, but if you need to refer to the past games to remind yourself, go ahead. Once you feel you are in your Full Body Listening and in the presence of your once-dysfunctional character, take your pen in your usual writing hand and communicate to it by writing:

Thank you so much for working so hard to support me all these years but I don't need that job done in that way any more. You can stand down.

Then, when you have finished, transfer your pen into your unusual writing hand and empty and empty and listen and listen, and even though it wasn't a question, before very long you will hear a response. Remember, you are not deliberately thinking anything up here, just listening deeply, and when you hear the character answer, your role is just to transcribe what you hear in your probably slightly wonky handwriting. Then, when you feel the response is complete and you've given it plenty of space, transfer the pen back into your usual writing hand, and ask:

Is there anything that you need?

Once again, transfer the pen back into your unusual writing hand and empty and empty and listen and listen, and whether it takes a few seconds or a couple of minutes, when you hear the response simply transcribe it. When you feel the response is complete and you have given it plenty of space, transfer the pen back into your usual writing hand, and ask:

Do you have a message for me?

Transcribe the character's answer in an unhurried and spacious fashion, until you are ready to ask the million-dollar question, again by writing with your usual writing hand: What new job could you now do instead that would be in harmony and in full support of how my life is now?

Take your time, listen deeply, and hear what idea this inner being offers up for serving and supporting you (which is all it has ever wanted to do since you created it).

Anything you want to ask a teacher, ask yourself, and wait for the answer in silence.

Byron Katie

When we are creating our projects and missions I like to think of each of us as building our own personal Evil Empire, having some fun including both our dark and light urges to manifest an entity which is authentic and drawing on all the available skills we have inside us. So, if you're getting a new mission together, the character we have just been playing with can be your first new employee. It used to be wandering around the building, misdirected, breaking the photocopier, but now, with its newly directed skills, it can be a helpful addition to whatever you are trying to achieve, both at work and in your relationships. Take a few minutes to come up with a funky new job title for this new staff member. Make it something groovy, even badass, something you would be proud to have on your business card. Some examples of job titles people have chosen on my weekends include:

Queen of Pleasure
Chief Executive of Courageousness
Cosmic Overseer
Chief CTU Field Operative/Bus Inspector
Brave Heart
Star Maker
Flip the Empowerment Switch
Kickass Healer

This technique is not only useful to gather vital data and direction from your demons, you can also interview parts of your body in the same way. If you have a repetitive problem that doesn't want to budge, use the same process to go softly into the listening field and ask the problem how it thinks it is trying to help you. What does it want to communicate that it needs to resort to such drastic measures to get your attention? What is its gift? What does it need?

All the genius is available to be sourced from our own deep

listening if we are willing to give it the space. I believe we are born with the innate skill to self-care in this way and it is only our culture's incorrect training that insists we have to keep looking elsewhere for the answers and get our problems fixed by other people. Of course, a genuine medical condition may need treatment, but there are often many steps we can take which could go a long way to participating in our genius body/mind's system of self-mending. Whatever other enquiries you feel you wish to make, ask away. My questions are just the beginning of a longer conversation if you want to go there. But before we move on, take a moment to tip your hat to your new employee and out loud, or in your mind, say, 'You're hired – welcome to the Evil Empire.'

THE BADGE GAME

This game goes to the core of our chronic self-editing. I don't want to give it too much of an introduction as it becomes clearer and clearer as it unfolds.

First, think of someone you really admire. This can be someone from your present or earlier life or anyone at all, whether you have met them or not. Pick someone who you feel lives life in the way you feel a yes to. Don't choose someone because of something great they did, rather it is how they live, how they operate in the world, their way of being. When you have chosen, write down their name on a piece of paper and then underneath write three adjectives about that person. Choose the three things which you love about them, the three aspects or qualities that you respect most about them. When you have written them down, pick the one quality from your chosen three that is the thing you most appreciate and admire about them, the one thing which really is so great about this person, and draw a circle around it.

Next, think of someone you don't admire, someone you don't respect, even dislike, and write their name below the last list. Again, list three adjectives about them underneath their name, the three things that are just so *ugh* about this person. Again, don't choose the person based on something awful they once did but rather how they roll, how they live their lives from your perspective. Then, when you have your three adjectives or qualities, draw a circle around the one thing which is just so repellent about them. Keep your Full Body Listening on as you do this and notice any sensations or feelings that arise during the process.

Now, on your paper you will have two words in circles. Take a look at them and allow a deep breath.

According to Joseph Campbell, Carl Jung, Robert Bly and many other wise thinkers . . . that is you. Those two words represent the polar reaches of your shadow self, two sides of you that you have given the least permission for in your life and remain shut-down, disembodied, and as Robert Bly says, qualities that we drag around in a sack behind us for our whole lives, hoping no one will see or disbelieving that those qualities could be us. But as humans, we are everything. We all carry generosity and greed, kindness and spite, authenticity and fakeness, surrender and control. It very much depends on how we have been brought up and the events that significantly impacted us as we grew up, which cocktail of qualities will be suppressed or amped up by the time we become adults. It may not always be appropriate to display our less socially acceptable qualities with no boundaries in our everyday lives but, as we have established, these parts of ourselves need somewhere they can be expressed and played with if we are to avoid unexpected leaks and self-sabotaging episodes where they force themselves out into the open to get a breath of air.

*

If you are in a group, you can now take a sticky label or a short strip of masking tape and write on it, large and legible, the negative of the two words you circled, and underneath, on the same name badge, write your first name. Stick the new shadow name sticker on your chest somewhere prominent. How does this feel? Are you grinning? Are you nervous? What is moving in you? What is being felt?

If it is just you and a partner or friend, you can still explore embodying your shadow character. Can you think about how aspects of this character affect your behaviour, perhaps even in the ways you try to suppress it.

The final stage of the game is to all stand up and move around the room embodying the one hundred and twenty per cent, totally unleashed expression of this 'negative' word. For as long as it feels fun and interesting, move around the space interacting with everyone else at least once, and short of causing physical pain to anyone, let the character named on your badge have full use of your body and voice. You may want to set some boundaries with the group before you play this part of the game. Some people might not be into getting shouted at, for instance, so check in with your gang before you get going. I also like to play some zany Czech oompah music along with the mayhem as it both encourages a mood of foolishness and the volume of the music gives the shyer members of the game a bit of emotional cover to get swallowed up in the chaos.

I like playing this game just before lunch break so that the group have the option of staying in character when they head out to the local cafés. Take the shadow theatre out onto the streets, I say! Before you leave this game, consider which areas of your life you could bring a little more flavour of this character to. Where can this aspect of you join the essence of mischief in your life? It is another great opportunity to, in an ongoing way, feed meat to the demons.

For me, I have applied to meet my own aggression. It has always been there, and it has a familiarity when it rears and rages, but I have never faced it soberly, explicitly acknowledged it exists and observed all its sudden, surging entrances and thinly veiled expressions.

I know I am aggressive in many ways. I am surgically aggressive with emails to people who I perceive are trying to be dishonest or unfair or disrespectful to me. I stress the word 'perceive' because there is often a difference between the perceived disrespect I'm reacting to and the actual disrespect being delivered. It is obvious that I am being seduced by a trigger into my aggression, that in the moment my anger feels completely justified in its self-righteous raging:

This person's an idiot.

This person is disrespecting me.

This person is trying to be dishonest with me.

When I receive an email from someone being judgemental about me or my work, when someone sends me an overtly or covertly bullying email, especially an indirect, sarcastic kind of message, I want to dissect and kill every syllable they wrote to me and spell out their hypocrisy and blindness to them in a way that *shows* them and silences them. I want to make them feel as dismissed as I feel.

I am trying to feel into this 'saying fuck off to bullies' attraction. I want to be metaphorically 'upstairs' as the high being who knows everyone is just a version of me, a lesson, a gift for me to lighten up and let go, and at the same time be metaphorically 'downstairs' as a human, primal in flesh and bone and say 'fuck off, you bully!' to those people so articulately that there is no room for anything but how *I* see it. This is aggressive. It's an aggressive way to protect the hurt I feel or the fear I feel in my body from old bullies of long ago.

And again, I also have to look at both my reaction and – how am I just like them? How do I lay my own superiority trips on people? Make them feel small so I can feel less threatened? Do I do that? How am I just like the smug, superior, dismissive bullies? I look at how I shame others, how I make them feel guilty for displeasing me as if they are wrong and responsible for how I now feel. Shaming people when they don't behave as I would prefer them to is aggression. I am examining my speech and my verbal tactics with my kids.

I don't want my unconsciously arising aggression to cause harm to anyone near me or to sabotage my life. So I applied to meet my aggression and the reply has been a cast of thousands – people and circumstances delivered by Almighty Productions both to trigger my own aggression so I can observe it and also send characters to mirror and mimic my own behaviours and strategies, so that I can see myself in Technicolor and tie bells to the ankles of my insidious traps – all the better to hear them coming sooner and not get sucker-punched so often.

I don't know if your own aggression feels out of proportion, or if it is another character or demon that it would now be a good time to meet. It is up to us as individuals to stop pushing these intense feelings under the surface only to watch them explode without warning over trivial things or, if not trivial, things that do not warrant us being so consumed and powerless in that moment when we are triggered. If we are going to make deeper and compassionate connections with others, we need first to be more compassionate and patient and loving towards ourselves.

Some believe that we somehow choose the map of all the things we are going to work on in this life and that all the most challenging people we encounter are in fact old soul friends who have made agreements with us to play the role of the abuser or enemy. The idea is that they will come into our lives deliberately to set up the conditions by which we are wounded, or challenged, to create our curriculum perfectly for this lifetime. The idea is that after you die you all get together and your best friend peels off the mask of your greatest enemy that he was wearing for that life and you congratulate him and thank him for doing the most amazing job at playing your toxic mother or hateful ex-husband or whatever, for being a genius cast member in your recent Earthworld experiment.

I know it sounds wacky, but there is a certain sense and grace to this theory. I have always felt that Judas was in on it somehow, or chosen by Jesus, as his closest friend, to be the only one he could depend upon to betray him. As someone once said, 'Only your best friends can really nail you up.' In the same way, it is our shadow characters who hold so much of our potential to live a fully creative and rich life. If we are willing to meet them in the here and now, we give ourselves the chance to transform them from demons into muses, and into our most creative employees.

CHAPTER 8

The Edge of Comfort

I want to stand as close to the edge as I can without going over. Out on the edge you see all the kinds of things you can't see from the center.

Kurt Vonnegut

The legendary Tibetan teacher Chögyam Trungpa Rinpoche says: 'A best friend is someone who insults you.' Why does he say this? Why does Ram Dass say 'suffering is grace'? It is because being so addicted to our safe and appropriate comfort zones is not satisfying us and is standing in the way of the riches and inspirations that Life has in store for us. The truth is that the edges of our comfort zone hold the treasures of discovery and re-empowerment, and unless we are willing to sometimes snorkel around our coastline, we are likely to plod along living lives which are far from our potential.

It is when we edit ourselves into a safe and 'appropriate' version that we limit ourselves to this comfort zone and there-fore massively limit our experience of Life. When we push down our demons we make ourselves and our world small. We let fear run the show and spend much of our energy just trying to keep a lid on things, let alone sailing out into unknown seas.

All the things and people which trigger us and make us feel those edges show us where we are still addicted and clinging in our lives. They show us a vivid menu of all the places where we are not accepting ourselves and treating ourselves with care. And so, as we begin to play with our demons and transform our shadows, we give ourselves the opportunity to explore those edges, to question our limiting and self-sabotaging beliefs, and to begin to welcome the lessons and gifts that Life is offering us, always in the most unexpected places.

This process does not need to be done traumatically. We are not meant to ignore all our sensitivities and boundaries and rush straight out into the deep water where we might drown, but neither does it befit our precious human existence to staunchly root ourselves as far away from any edges as we can, and fight and scream and complain any time Life offers us a more coastal experience. There is no escaping it: the walls we put up to 'protect' ourselves will inevitably imprison us. All security is an illusion. Surrender is the only option.

LETTING GO OF LABELS

Something that has helped me immensely as I navigate life's dramas is the practice of removing the label from the feelings that come up. I might be driving along, thinking about something painful from the recent events of my life, and a wave of grief or loss hits me. Usually, at that moment I will start thinking about the events and stir up the feelings even more by feeding them. This is an unconscious technique to try and control the uncomfortable sensations which I'm feeling, but by labelling the feelings, for example 'grief' or 'loss', I have so many preconceptions and negative associations around those labels my system will react automatically before I've even allowed myself to feel them fully. I'm having a past-infused version of these intense waves which I have already coloured with the belief that 'grief and loss are things we don't want', all because of the labels I'm automatically attaching to those waves passing through me. My new experiment has been to remove those labels and simply experience the intense waves as a neutral, unnamed sensation, as if I'm having it for the first time and I have no preconceptions about it. Sometimes I give it a meaningless name like 'Oh, I'm feeling *schlumph*'. It is extraordinary how quickly the experience of those waves transforms when I remove the accustomed labels.

This practice helps me to be fully willing to feel whatever is going on in me, even when challenging. I have experimented with taking it a step further, exploring and even relabelling the sensation as Love. What if this sensation was one of the millions of diverse versions of Love? Suddenly, the power we all have to define our experiences, either positively or negatively, simply by how we decide to frame whatever's going on, is becoming more and more achievable; it is becoming fascinating to feel these waves as if for the first time, without cloaking them in the usually assumed tragedy.

> Tender heart of sadness: This sadness doesn't come from being mistreated. You don't feel sad because someone has insulted you or because you feel impoverished. Rather, this experience of sadness is unconditioned. It occurs because your heart is

completely open, exposed. It is the pure raw heart. Even if a
mosquito lands on it, you feel so touched . . . It is this tender
heart of a warrior that has the power to heal the world.

Chögyam Trungpa Rinpoche

Noticing that all the things which trigger you identify places
where you are lacking permission or self-acceptance is a golden
opportunity, a chance to be powerful where once you were disempowered and reactive. If you are ready for a brave adventure you
might not only meet the unexpected episodes this way, you might
even go hunting. It takes a hardcore seeker to embark upon such
a quest and actively seek out the unprocessed, reactive areas of
your psyche and body which are yet to be invited home, rather
than wait for them to present themselves in a crisis, but it means
you can set in place the support you need to address those shadows
ahead of time and choose an efficient method *before* you are
knocked for six.

It goes without saying that this is an area which requires total
commitment to self-care. It is not a place to be over-bold, or
push yourself further than your boundaries allow. Deciding to
journey into the darkest realms of the forest needs preparation
and realism, not bravado. When we choose practices that take
us to our edges we need to secure support so that we can be held
and contained should unexpectedly mighty waves crash down on
us. But journeying into these places willingly with the right
people supporting you is one of the greatest gifts you can ever
give yourself.

Here are a couple of games which go a little deeper. They
both liberate frozen creative gifts and release us from old,
tangled-up tripwires which might have been limiting us for years

without our knowledge. If you are going to try them out, be extra gentle with yourself.

THE COURTROOM GAME

There's a wonderful fairytale about a magical wishing tree called 'Wishes' written by . . . OK, it's written by me, but it's still a good story . . . and one of the main characters is a queen who begins to look at her beauty as a curse and to distrust the surface appearance of things.

The Queen herself was so exquisitely beautiful that any man who came to court her was immediately struck dumb in her presence. He would stumble over his ill-chosen words in vain attempts to impress her. He would gloat and boast and exaggerate his accomplishments and often find himself clumsily lying to astonish her. This Queen was also deeply wise, and these bumbling fools left her melancholy and tired. All she yearned for was a true connection – some open-hearted laughter, a profound conversation – and yet each strutting courtier was a greater disappointment than the last, and none of them once discovered the fragile grace that resided in her heart.

One of her many duties as regent of her queendom was to preside over the disputes of her subjects and this was never her favourite occupation. To endure having to sit through the petty squabbles of farmers and merchants bored her to tears and ate into her horse-riding time, so she had a method that was both wise and time saving. As soon as she felt the two conflicting parties had reached an impasse she would summon them both

to her throne and command them, on pain of death, to return
the next morning and argue their opponent's case to the best of
their ability, and she would warn them that if she felt either of
them weren't trying their absolute hardest to convince her of
their opponent's innocence and the righteousness of their position
and argument, she would have whoever wasn't trying hard enough
put to death and all their lands and possessions given to their
enemy. Unsurprisingly, agreements were soon reached.

For this game, you need to first choose an episode from your
past which was never fully cleared or resolved. Choose a painful
falling out with someone who never apologised or admitted the
truth of what happened. Don't choose something that 'happened
to you' as a child, an abusive experience. Better to choose
something from when you were an adult or late teenager onwards.
I am asking you to choose a situation that never had closure,
where basically you were right and they were wrong, and the
justice and mutual acknowledgement of what really happened
was never arrived at. This might be a drama that played out
with someone who is now gone from your life, maybe you don't
talk any more because of it, or maybe they died, or perhaps
they are still in your life but it is a subject that you both steer
clear of.

I would like you now to reconnect to that episode, the feeling
of it, not the details and events, and with your Full Body
Listening on, sit for a few minutes allowing the flavour of that
time to return and be felt. You might even lay a hand on the
place in your body which is being activated, staying present
with your breath and noticing yourself in all ways.

Your task now for this game is to write, in bullet-point form,
so you can argue it clearly in your own words, the case for the

---

defence for the person you fell out with. I suggest the following structure:

List 1) You have to bring any and all possible reasons for their behaviour which might shed a light of innocence on their part in what happened back then. You have to do this without falsifying the evidence. This isn't a game where we make up things which aren't true, but you can speculate on any state of mind or ignorance or other past formative experiences that they might have gone through which could lend any understanding to or forgiveness for their actions.

List 2) The second list, also in bullet-point form, is for you to explain and argue all the ways that you yourself played your part in what happened. NB This does not mean blaming yourself or making it all your fault. This list is to acknowledge anything you did or did not do, anything you were naive about, any signs that you missed, or any way at all that your state of being at the time might have facilitated what happened. Include ideas on how, had you conducted yourself differently or been more aware, the situation might have played out differently. I repeat, this is not a self-blaming exercise; it is a way to include the parts we all play in such episodes and be unvarnished about all sides of what happened.

List 3) This part is optional but potent. Usually in our retelling of these stories we have honed the version of events to such a patter that one or two vital pieces of evidence, often ones which lessen the one-sidedness of the tale, or even undermine our own position completely, seem to accidentally-on-purpose fall by the wayside. I'm suggesting that there might be at least one piece of information – maybe it is something that only you know, or something you never include in the telling of the story – that would ruin the whole effect of injustice.

If this does exist, I dare you to write it down. Is there anything at all that you leave out when you tell a new person about the injustice of those events?

Spend at least half an hour to reflect on all this. It takes a lot of courage to revisit the more painful episodes of our lives with fresh eyes and minds. There is a kind of safety in sticking to the times where we were unarguably the victim, and the few examples we have of this in our lives can be very hard to give up, but they are prisons of our own architecture, and while we don't want to pretend we were to blame when someone else acted unjustly, our attachment to such events has far-reaching, limiting effects on our ability to be powerful in the world.

When you've completed your three lists, find a partner you trust or a small group and, having contextualised the story of what happened, proceed to use every argument at your disposal to convince them of every item on your lists. Their job is to hold a listening container for you and, if necessary, police you in your full commitment to the truth of what you're sharing.

Some questions it's worth asking yourself:

In what slightly delicious way have I been enjoying being in the right?

What is the bravest, most healing and progressive action I could now take regarding this story?

What was the gift or training buried within this experience?

Is there anything I've missed or skipped?

This is one of those games where you might unexpectedly feel a well of emotion rise up, both in the reliving of the upsetting circumstances, but also the regrets at one's own conduct, then and since, and the relief at putting down a heavy bag that is only a burden to ourselves. I once interviewed Carrie Fisher about forgiveness for the second 1 Giant Leap film and my favourite quote of the day was: 'Holding onto resentments is like drinking poison and hoping someone else is going to die.'

THE NAUGHTY STEP GAME

This is another edgy game and includes an idea that may be the hardest one to entertain or consider in the whole book.

OK, to start us off, I'd like you to connect to a time in your life when you got caught or screwed up badly, or maybe just went along with others and got caught up in an event that went horribly wrong. Whatever you choose, the important thing is for it to be a time when you felt memorably shamed, either by someone else or yourself, and you still remember the impact of that shame. As usual, I recommend turning on your Full Body Listening to drop into this one.

OK, now for the edgy concept. Open your mind to the following: Could it be that every action, no matter how indefensible, began as a positive impulse?

To explore this idea we need to divide the actions that took place from the root impulses that spawned them, in the same way the Rudolf Steiner meditation invites us to first hear the sound of a baby crying or the sound of a dog barking but then tune in to the impulse that threw that sound out, the root spark that originally caused that sound to come forth. Here we are separating the 'bad' action from the first moment the birth of that person's involvement in the story led to the 'bad' action.

From where I sit, no matter what terrible choices were made or heinous crimes committed, the original attraction or intention that preceded it was always positive.

Let's take a totally standard, indefensible action like stealing money from a charity box to spend on chocolates at the sweet shop. Of course, on the surface, there is no excuse for that action, but I am not defending actions in this game. I am separating them from the first feeling or thought that birthed them, the feeling that arose before stupid or harmful choices were made. There is a space between having an attraction or inspiration and then making ill-advised decisions which lead to disaster. Taking the charity box example, if we zoom in with a microscope and divide the thieving from the first impulse that birthed it happening, we notice that before any foolhardy plan was hatched to steal from the charity box, the initial inspiration was 'Wouldn't it be great if my friends and I could have enough money to buy all the sweets and chocolates we wanted and all share a scarcity-free experience of abundance together!', which, to me, is a totally healthy and excitingly abundant idea. The actions that followed were dishonest and antisocial, but the moment when the idea arose was clean. Stay with me here, this is going somewhere . . .

Another example, let's go further. Let's say . . . chopping up your ex-wife and her lover with an axe. On the face of it, not a very nice thing to do. Yes, the action of going round to their house and murdering them is wrong, but using the same exercise of dividing actions from first impulses we have to acknowledge that the initial thought of 'I am going crazy with jealously and abandonment. I need to do something to end this torment!' is a totally legitimate and self-caring first step. The actions that the violently driven and probably insane person then took with the axe are of course horrific. I just want to illustrate here, for reasons which may become apparent later in the game, that the initial spark for nearly any terrible action you can come up with is always positive.

For the next stage of the game, take a few minutes to reflect on the shaming incident you have chosen to play with and consider what was the first moment or impulse of intention before any actions were chosen. For instance, I have often hurt people's feelings by blurting out something insensitive. When I drop in to those moments I discover that my first impulse was 'This will be really funny and edgy and create intimacy and we'll all laugh together and feel great!' Sadly, I didn't then check in clearly enough to consider that my words might not land as hilariously as they first sounded in my head, so the action that followed created upset and then, for me, some shame and regret. Sometimes hurting someone's feelings can come from a poorly executed need to feel less disempowered or stand up for oneself. Sometimes hurtful or dishonest actions can come from a desperate need to protect one's own sensitivities or hide from something scary. Let yourself explore and wonder about the episode that you chose for this game and see if you can determine one or more positive intentions or gifts that seemed like a good idea before you chose some possibly regrettable actions.

This is where we get support from our partner or group when playing with others. Sit down with each other and not only discuss the difference between your first impulse and the choices that followed, but once you have uncovered the originally intended gift(s) also ask yourself: how is that initial gift or positivity operating in my life now?

With my blurting, thinking-it's-funny-but-it-isn't moments, I have discovered that the root impulse was 'making everyone laugh and feeling togetherness', so I ask myself, Jamie, how is your gift of 'making everyone laugh and feeling togetherness' operating in your life today? Will I never attempt to make everyone laugh and feel togetherness because what happened was so painful that I've shut down that whole gift for fear of reliving the agony *or* am I compulsively trying over and over to make everyone laugh and feel togetherness, being funny in front of groups every weekend who think they're on a workshop, making edgy observations on Facebook and with whoever I'm with, as a massive over-compensation for what happened in the past? Usually you will find that whatever gift(s) you have come up with connected to this shamed episode you will either have shut it down or blown it out of proportion. Somehow, in these shaming moments the originally intended gift to ourselves or others got warped in the process and either squashed or magnified, and that essential gift that lives in you, until recalibrated, is not functioning healthily any more. Are you over-doing it or under-doing it these days?

While you are discussing your experience with your partner or group don't forget to cover both sides of the question:

What was the originally intended, positive outcome or gift when this first entered my life?

How is that gift operating in my life today?

Always keep your Full Body Listening on while chatting about it so that if your body/mind genius needs to move some emotion or redistribute some sensation in you, you are right there feeling it in the moment and giving it your full, self-caring, spacious presence. In the final stage, invite in that younger, shamed you in whatever way feels natural. You're getting used to this now, so you might find that connecting to this inner character happens more naturally than the last couple of times. Either way, once you feel you are in the presence of the shamed character, you are ready, with pen and paper, to begin a conversation.

As before, ask or write to the character with the pen in your usual writing hand and then transfer the pen to your unusual writing hand and listen and listen and empty and empty for the answer and just transcribe what you hear from them with your slower, wonky handwriting.

First, we write and ask the character:

Would you like to rejoin me?

Making this consensual and an invitation is the most gentle way to approach this dialogue. When you have transferred the pen and transcribed the first answer, continue the dialogue with the same usual hand/unusual hand technique to ask the following questions:

Was there anything unjust about what happened, then or since?

What was the gift you intended for yourself or others?

How would you most like to bring and express that gift in my life now?

You can ask further questions and allow the conversation to unfold in any way which feels natural to you. These are just my starter questions, the essentials to unfreeze that gift in your life, like cashing in chips at the casino. It can be useful to think of one or more concrete ways that feel attractive to commit to bringing that gift back, maybe one way to give it to yourself and one way to give it to others. Feel what it feels like to be free to uncage that quality in your life. Is there any resistance still? If so, allow it to dissolve in the body. Listen to its beliefs. Welcome it home.

The key concept to allow to emerge here is your essential innocence. Even if you 'did something terrible' and even if you need to soberly address what ignorance or fears made you choose to give that gift in a way that ended up creating shame and upset, it's vital not to allow that mistake to freeze up that gift in your life for ever. Can you get in touch with any level of your innocence here? Can you give yourself a break? Can you cut yourself some slack for the imperfect way you conducted yourself? Or maybe you were acting perfectly and just found yourself in the line of fire of someone who didn't understand where you were really coming from. Being misunderstood can be a huge source of shame and gift paralysis. It's time to invite that gift-bearing character off the naughty step and dare to practise giving that gift again freely in your life.

When we encourage ourselves to gently explore these difficult experiences, we begin to dissolve the barriers that keep us from venturing beyond our comfort zone. It turns out that the demons and monsters we thought had been banished, and that scare us from entering the shadows, have been with us all along. When we let the barriers and walls dissolve, we begin to see their gifts and discover treasure where once we saw only guilt and shame.

> The bad news is you're falling through the air, nothing to hang on to, no parachute. The good news is there's no ground.
>
> Chögyam Trungpa Rinpoche

CHAPTER 9

Suffering for Love

Hezekiah: Ahh. Very passable, this, eh, very passable.

Obadiah: Nothing like a good glass of Chateau de Chassilier eh, Josiah?

Josiah: Aye, you're right there, Obadiah.

Ezekiel: Who'd a thought thirty years ago we'd all be sittin' here drinking Chateau de Chassilier, eh?

H: Aye. In them days, we'd a' been glad to have the price of a cup o' tea.

O: A cup o' COLD tea.

E: Without milk or sugar.

J: OR tea!

H: In a cracked cup and all.

E: We never used to have a cup. We used to have to drink out of a rolled-up newspaper.

O: The best WE could manage was to suck on a piece of damp cloth.

J: But you know, we were happy in those days, although we were poor.

H: BECAUSE we were poor. My old dad used to say to me, 'Money doesn't bring you happiness, son.'

E: 'E was right. I was happier then and I had NOTHIN'. We used to live in this tiny old tumbledown house, with great big holes in the roof.

O: House? You were lucky to live in a HOUSE! We used to live in one room, all twenty-six of us, no furniture. Half the floor was missing; we were all huddled together in one corner for fear of FALLING!

J: You were lucky to have a ROOM! *We* used to have to live in the corridor!

H: Oh we used to DREAM of livin' in a corridor! Woulda' been a palace to us. We used to live in an old water tank on a rubbish tip. We got woke up every morning by having a load of rotted fish dumped all over us! House!? Hmph.

E: Well when I say 'house' it was just a hole in the ground covered by a sheet of tarpaulin, but it was a house to US.

O: We were evicted from *our* hole in the ground; we had to go and live in a lake!

J: You were lucky to have a LAKE! There were a hundred and fifty of us living in a shoebox in the middle of the road.

H: Cardboard box?

J: Aye.

H: You were lucky. We lived for three months in a rolled-up newspaper in a septic tank. We used to have to get up every morning at six o'clock, clean the newspaper, go to work down mill for fourteen hours a day week in-week out for sixpence a week. And when we got home, our dad would thrash us to sleep with his belt!

O: Luxury. We used to have to get out of the lake at three o'clock in the morning, clean the lake, eat a handful of hot gravel, work twenty hours a day at mill for tuppence a month, come home, and Dad would beat us around the neck with a broken bottle, if we were LUCKY!

J: Well of course we had it tough. We used to have to get up out of the shoebox in the middle of the night, and LICK the road clean with our tongues. We had to eat half a handful of freezing cold gravel, worked twenty-four hours a day at the mill for fourpence every six years, and when we got home, our dad would slice us in two with a bread knife.

E: Right. I had to get up in the morning at ten o'clock at night, half an hour before I went to bed (pause for laughter), eat a lump of cold poison, work twenty-nine hours a day down mill, and pay mill owner for permission to come to work, and when we got home, our dad would kill us, and dance about on our graves singing 'Hallelujah'.

H: But you try and tell the young people today that . . . and they won't believe ya'.

ALL: Nope, nope.

'The Four Yorkshiremen' sketch, Monty Python's Flying Circus

Something that puzzles me is how often we hide our true pain while, at the same time, we elevate our *complaints* to one of the most valuable currencies we use to get what we want. It's as if the more we play the martyr, the more we deserve love and care. Once again, this is a result of that strange club that sprung up after Jesus died. Don't get me wrong, I have nothing against Jesus. The man, or the idea of the man, who came to encourage everyone to open their hearts and love each other is a beautiful thing. It is strange, though, how the Christian Church has treated his story. You would think the church would be all about releasing the healing power of Christ into the world, wouldn't you? Yet what symbol do they use as the main image to bow to and wear around their necks? When you bow to something you say yes to it, you energise it, so of all the beautiful and inspiring images they could have chosen from the Jesus stories, all the wonderful things he is said to have done like feeding the five thousand, healing the sick, raising Lazarus from the dead, walking on water, it is a bit odd to me that the image chosen to be praised and empowered is the one and only time in the story where Jesus is brutalised, humiliated, disempowered, nailed up and even, in some versions of the story, when he lost his own faith for a moment – 'My God, why have you forsaken me?'

Everyone bows to the image of the cross, to that concept of suffering and disempowerment. It is almost as if the church wants to freeze the power of Christ, not encourage it. In this club, the highest attainment is to become a saint, and what do you have to do to be a saint? Perform a miracle . . . oh, and die a martyr's death. If you die painfully and unjustly then you are elevated to the highest seat in the house. Generation after generation of this model has left our culture believing that suffering is worthy, suffering makes you special. It is an interesting question to ask: 'Would God, or Life, love me just as much if I had no suffering at all?' Do we deserve the same amount of love and care when we are not suffering? If we believe suffering makes us more deserving of love then we are all going to unconsciously create more and more suffering in our lives to attract the love we need. It is a bit like the child who realises that it gets much more attention from its parents when it hurts itself so it keeps, accidentally-on-purpose, falling over in the playground or developing symptoms of illness.

This is not the same as witnessing our suffering and pain and using it to see where we are clinging and where we truly need support or can give support to another. It is when we fall into unconsciously milking it for drama or sympathy that we use our suffering as a currency in exchange for love. Notice how much you and the people around you push their suffering stories and, conversely, share your joys and victories less, as if it's boasting, as if by sharing what is good will result in less love or even some sort of rejection.

We use our suffering to get what we want. For instance, a couple with a baby:

She: Darling, would you change this nappy? I've done the last five.

He: Done the last five? I've been working the last ten hours!

She: Working the last ten hours? I've been up with him the last ten nights!

Suddenly we're playing martyr tennis, back and forth, topping each other, and whoever wins gets their own way.

When you get to work and say 'Oh, the traffic was *terrible!*' and someone immediately replies 'Oh, let me make you a cup of tea', it is as though you just earned that cup of tea with your little suffering offering.

When we volunteer our suffering stories without first checking that the listener wants to hear them or give us their support we are indirectly eliciting their care without permission. People are immediately triggered into offering care or sympathy before they have been directly asked for support, and this both promotes the culture of suffering and pulls on everyone's energy without them being in on it. We all do this from time to time, and some employ this underhanded method for getting attention all day long, because it works! We are all so invested in suffering being worthy, the currency of deserving love, that we fall into constant conversations about how hard everything is.

Now, I'm not saying we don't need or deserve support from one another, but to get it by pushing the suffering card, instead of daring to be vulnerable and directly asking for it, can be deceitful and vampy (I mean vampiric here, not that we're putting on eyeliner and burlesque gear). Over the years of running my Transforming Shadows groups we have built up a long list of all the ways we use our suffering to get attention and care. Some are subtle, some are flagrant. At first, everyone laughs smugly, sure that of course it's *those other people* that do this, not them, but as we go through the list, smiles of sheepish recognition spread throughout the group. So here is the list. I suggest writing down any of the manipulations that you use sometimes (or often) so you can play with them later. Playfulness is the key to dissolving these unconscious patterns. To me, playfulness is the core foundation of wisdom.

So here goes . . . how many of these do you do?

1) Looking upset until they notice.
2) Going on about how tired you are and how little sleep you've had.
3) Complaining about how much you've given but not had fairly reciprocated.
4) Complaining about costs and money.
5) Looking flustered, like *I'm going to freak out in a minute!*

6) Obviously false ways you say 'I'm fine' or tell people 'No, no, it's all right' when it clearly isn't.

7) Using the phrase 'not too bad' when someone asks you how you are.

8) Putting yourself down.

9) Refusing help.

10) Not asking for help and then getting annoyed about not getting it.

11) Communicating through a tense tone of voice.

12) Begging and looking pathetic (one of my favourites).

13) Pushing the disempowerment card and making yourself smaller and needier.

14) Being habitually unfairly misunderstood.

15) Complaining about parts of your body or your looks.

16) Sighing and making sad sounds.

17) Playing down what a great time you're having.

18) Refusing compliments.

19) Comparing yourself or our circumstances unfavourably with other people's.

20) Going on about how much you have to do and how little time to do it.

21) Wheeling out stories of your sad childhood and wearing the heavy things you endured as if they are a badge of honour and credibility.

22) Complaining about the opposite sex.

23) Over-eating or over-drinking, making yourself sick, and then whining to everyone about it.

24) Exaggerating how bad something was.

25) Using the phrase 'you don't know what it's like'.

26) Feeling let down by other's lack of telepathy. *(Ladies!)*

27) Going on about how much better things were before.

28) Ranting, assuming everyone needs to hear your angrily expressed woes.

Another little manipulation that I am going to add here is when we give reasons for asking for help. When someone asks you a favour and then adds 'because I haven't had a day off all week', they are lessening your right to say no by dialling up their suffering. It may sound harsh, but we need to check in ourselves when asking for help. Are the reasons we offer simply an explanation or manipulation?

If you would like to dissolve these manipulative strategies for getting love and care without vulnerably and directly asking for it, then there is a fun game you can play, either in front of the mirror alone (preferably filming yourself on your smartphone) or, even better, in groups.

The Suffering for Love Game

Go through the list and choose a few of the suffering strategies listed that you employ and then do an exaggerated impression of yourself doing it. It is hilarious to witness yourself in this mode and crack everyone up with the outrageousness of the manipulation. The more you exaggerate it, the freer of the strategy you become. Really let in the foolishness. Allow what used to be your pulling on people's unconscious giving response to transform into entertainment and liberation.

If you are playing this game with others, the listener's role while you act out your manipulative strategy, sharing your faux

---

suffering with your playmates, is to give you as much fake sympathy as they can, totally buying in to your suffering. Sympathetic phrases like 'oh, that's terrible' and 'you're so brave' and 'you're a saint, you really are' work very well. You may even try joining them in their suffering . . . 'oh yes, I've had exactly the same thing with my husband' or even try and top their suffering with your own, as if you are one of the four Yorkshiremen in the Monty Python sketch – 'Pain? You don't know the meaning of the word, I had it much worse' – and enjoy competing for the suffering crown.

I must add that this game comes with a Government Health Warning. Once you have played it, it seems so appallingly obvious how many people are trading off this suffering currency and pulling on you day after day that you can easily get quite judgemental and intolerant of their behaviour. It seems so obvious, but remember that all this stuff is habitual and unconscious, so don't judge others too harshly. That doesn't mean you have to put up with it, though, and if you notice certain people who do little else but communicate through these suffering strategies I think it can be wise and self-caring to take distance, even if they are immediate family members. No one is required to show up for being sucked on, so unless you enjoy offering yourself up as a sacrificial lamb to their misery, it is sensible to make boundaries for yourself and limit the exposure to the vampires in your life.

Don't forget how easy it is to become an enabler. Many of us (me included) get energy from playing along with other people's dramas. It can feel good to be the one who 'cares' while someone is self-indulgently whining.

Some people need you to keep being an addict so they can
keep mopping up your puke and feel needed.

(ancient Brooklyn proverb)

Dissolving these suffering-for-love strategies is central to living
a creative and intimate life. It creates intimacy to reach out to
others for support in a more honest and vulnerable way. Every
time we manipulate to get the connection we crave we are limiting
intimacy, we are hiding. In our all-consuming self-involvement
we are massively limiting our capacity for genuine compassion.
This focus on lack creates more lack. If we want to experience
our lives fully, vividly, intensely in this short human life we have
been given, then daring to be visible in our needs, daring to ask
for what we need authentically is a huge cultivator of the true
connection we all desire. It takes discipline to express gratitude
for what we have instead of sinking into self-pity, but whatever
we focus on is what will play out in our lives. As the old saying
goes, *when the pickpocket sees the Messiah walking down the street all
he sees are His pockets.*

However we frame what is happening to us determines our
experience of it. If we see it as a lack, we will experience lack.
If we see it as a possible lesson or illumination, we become
powerful, oh, and please, when you hear me complaining about
something, don't remind me of my hypocrisy in the situation,
it totally messes with my flow.

CHAPTER 10

Unleashing the Genius

What am I in the eyes of most people? A good-for-nothing, an eccentric and disagreeable man, somebody who has no position in society and never will have. Very well, even if that were true, I should want to show by my work what there is in the heart of such an eccentric man, of such a nobody.

Vincent van Gogh

I always find it a little strange when you consider that everything we humans have made, not just the paintings and sculptures and music but all the medicine and the light fittings and the tyres and trampolines, *all* began as a spark in someone's imagination. All that happened next was a series of *actions* all in a row, and then at the end of the line the new thing existed. But given that it is the *imagination realm* that creates for us all technology, all architecture, all machinery, everything we wear, all our essential and non-essential things, that is, *everything* that isn't creatures, plants and rocks, you would think that it might be given more priority in the education and preparation of our kids than a few hours with some acrylic paint of a Friday afternoon supervised by a sensitive teacher on the verge of a nervous breakdown, no?

The irony is that all these *things* come from a space we know little about; there isn't a set formula for teaching people how to access their imagination and creativity. And often, it is those who struggle with formal education who find it easier to stay connected with the imagination realm as they grow up. Steve Jobs dropped out of college after only six months and travelled to India, where it was Zen Buddhism that introduced him to the power of imagination and intuition. Albert Einstein didn't speak until he was four or read until he was seven, and he was expelled from school and couldn't even get into Zürich Polytechnic College. What they both had was an unusual level of access to the imagination realm, a channel receptive to ideas and inspiration when you are willing to feel and be open to what might come.

When we are clear and free from all the beliefs that say *we can't do it* or *we're not good enough* or *it's too risky to expose ourselves* then the channel of all our abundant ideas and inspirations opens effortlessly. There is no genius that we have to insert to make you a great creator. You may need to learn some techniques if your medium requires skills such as knowing how to play the guitar, learn the lines, throw the clay on the wheel, or get a degree from Harvard Business School, but these are just tools; they are there to facilitate the 'form' that your natural genius takes but they aren't the juice itself.

Everyone has an abundance of genius that has been often squashed or demotivated or left uncultivated. The thing that excites and attracts you is the clearest map to what your own unique gift is. If you haven't practised your Full Body Listening it is likely that you won't be embodied enough or spacious enough to even know what truly excites you. You might go off down a path which you think other people would approve of, or might look easy and undemanding, but unless it is driven by the urge of excitement and attraction there is little chance the bigger genius which is available in the listening field beyond your thinking mind will get a chance to come through.

This is why we have spent the majority of this book making sure we are in a clear and awake enough state to be undistracted by the constant doubts and triggers and distractions. It is only when we are in our power, lifted out of our usual unconscious and reactive dramas that are crowding out the present moment, that we have a hope of being available for a Masterpiece, whether it be art, a relationship or being alone with ourselves.

DO WHAT EXCITES YOU

My experience is that this creative channel only opens when I am really *into it*. When I am totally consumed with the idea or the excitement of the mission, of the potential and possibilities, then I will have a chance to produce something really great. In that space, in that excitement, you can't stop me, I am *taken by it*. I have endless energy and I barely need to eat. It is like my body is making its own vitamins. Yet when I am tasked to do something which doesn't turn me on, it feels almost impossible to drag myself to it: the work will suffer, I will try to get it out of the way quickly yet probably deliver it late, and I will eat tons of crap to distract and reward myself just to get through it. Doing things which don't inspire us is unhealthy. Working or creating from that place produces substandard results and uses up so much more energy that it becomes unsustainable. When we work, create or relate from this place we also feel terrible about ourselves. We see the poor-quality results and begin to believe that we have lost it, that the doors of creative flow are closed to us, and this all comes from agreeing to expend energy and time on things which don't feel attractive. This is why one of my golden rules for unleashing the genius is: *Never do any parts of your project that don't feel fun to you.*

There is always someone who is excited to do the roles and jobs that you're not into. When I make some music the last thing I want to do is run into the live room to move the microphone a quarter of an inch next to the amplifier and run back into the control room to check the minutia of the bass sound, but there are many technical engineer types, many great producers and artists, who live for that shit, and don't get me wrong, recording things beautifully is essential in the process. I just don't have any interest in being that guy, so in order to work how I work I always make sure to invite a genius technical engineer to partner up with me and usually give them half of the whole project because their role is so fundamental. The only thing that is important is that the finished piece sounds incredible. I am devotional to the project or the song or whatever it is, and if that means having to give away half or even more shares of the money it is going to make to other people, so be it.

It is better to have five per cent of something that does incredibly well than ninety-five per cent of something that does OK.

When you are consumed by a project or piece of art you are as much of an usher as a creator, constantly listening to the thing you are working on and responding to its needs. You are like a gardener. You don't exactly invent the tomato plant but you create the most healthy environment for it to thrive as you can. Parenting is no different. We don't, hopefully, impose on the child what he or she is going to be. We provide the most nurturing environment for them to discover their own gifts and passions. It is only by being in our Full Body Listening that the intuitive relationship between me and my art (or my partner, or my children) can occur and the chance of a Masterpiece appearing can be optimised. This is why the first question I ask when someone is choosing their mission or project is: *If you had all your life expenses paid for, what do you really want to do after breakfast?*

When someone tells me 'I want to be in films', I usually raise one eyebrow and ask 'do you want to get up at crazy o'clock in the morning and turn up at shoots in the freezing cold eating weird bacon rolls and sitting next to editors ploughing through hours of footage you're not going to use . . . or do you just love the idea of being at the premiere and standing at the podium thanking your mum and the Academy?' It's the *process* of the project you have to be excited about, not the end product, because once we get started, the end product can be a nebulous thing. This is where one of the great paradoxes of creativity comes in. It is important to have a really clear vision, but a flexible one. That means you work diligently towards the best clear vision you have so far while being totally open to it turning into an even better clear vision at any moment. This is the listening, this is the surrender that Life requires.

We are doing it because we love doing it, we love the process. Whether you give us £1,000 to do it or £1 million, *we're doing it anyway.* The feeling of being absorbed and excited by a project or piece of art is what drives us, and it is the best and only compass for whether we are choosing the right area to dedicate our precious energy. Trust what turns you on. Make your projects according to your own taste and trust there are enough other people like you who will share it.

I remember as a kid, me and my pal Phil used to play in his grandmother's garden in Kent and construct inventions from the debris in her shed. One summer we decided to make a go-cart out of bits of a broken pram and some other crates and foraged findings. We were fully absorbed in it for a couple of days and really hoped it would fly along when we had finished, but whether it did or just fell to pieces on the first run was not a deal-breaker for whether we were going to be totally dedicated to our invention or not. (By the way, it did fly, it was awesome.) We can never put the burden of it *doing well* or *being successful* on the shoulders of a piece of art or a mission. It is a mystery how our projects are going to turn out and whether anyone will like them. That cannot be the ultimate motivation. Only loving what we are doing while we are doing it will imbue the work with something authentic and heartfelt that will touch those who are exposed to it when it is done. The rule that I believe everyone should nail above the door comes again from Bashar: 'Take action based on your excitement with no attachment to outcome.'

That second part is so important. If you think your time will be wasted on a project if it doesn't get well received at the end or make enough money, then you are choosing the wrong project. The success of the thing at the end is only an added bonus. Yes, we certainly *prefer* that it does brilliantly and we get awards and acclaim and lots of lovely feedback, but this is not a proviso to its having been a totally fulfilling and worthwhile use of our time.

The complexities that have all to fall into place for a project to be successful are incalculable. The quality, timing, the climate of what is getting airplay or media attention at the time, how the thousands of individuals exposed to it might be feeling on the day they heard it, the relationships between marketeers and distributors, broadcasters and retailers – having success with a project is like rolling a fifty-sided dice. You have no idea, even with a decent marketing budget and an experienced team, *no idea* if it is going to do well. If there was a formula then we would have it by now. The only fail-safe method I can offer is the total absorption and devotion to the project, because when we are driven by enjoyment and self-fulfilment in our work, every day we show up is abundant and worthwhile even if it flops when we release it.

This is extra true for folks like me who teach, mentor and run workshops. If I have a need for you to *get it* then I am not really giving to you. I am using you to feel *got*. If I think I know better than you how deep you should go or how much of a shift you should make at my workshops, then that is for me not you. I just offer the food and trust that everyone will eat as much as feels right for them. I have no idea if you need a mouthful or three bowls full. It's none of my business. If I am valuing myself based on how much everyone seemed to eat then I am using the diners to make me feel worthy. This is a huge trap and reverses the giving into a taking process. When I run a workshop I know some people will want to just meet it as an intellectual exercise, have some fun with the games and go home thinking, that was interesting, and there will be others who use it to go deep and maybe shift a block or a loop that has been hurting them for years. If I attach to one outcome more than the other I am asking for trouble. We cook the food. We serve the food. We don't get hung up on how much of it everyone wants to eat.

UNLEASHING INTIMACY

This is not to say that we have no connection with others when we make a project or a piece of art; it is that we do not enter into the process with an attachment to the outcome. We don't choose to do things so that we will be loved as a consequence, but the consequence of doing what we love is an opening up to genuine intimacy with no strings attached. We put ourselves and our gifts out there, in all our raw and vulnerable glory. And so the feeling of having our gifts received is bliss. The feeling of being allowed to be generous without having to hold back is fulfilment.

ACTUALLY DOING IT

OK, now having been as thorough as we can be that we have the capacity to listen deeply enough, spaciously enough, to receive inspirations and ideas which really turn us on, when we have been cultivating the more *feminine* aspects of our nature to allow in something more unexpected and limitless than what our thinking minds can come up with, it is finally time to get busy and unleash our powerful manifesting masculine powers upon the project. You have listened deeply to what excites you and you're now ready to take *action*.

YOUR SEVEN SAMURAI

No matter how solitary your project may seem, every mission needs a team. Even a book that you are writing alone needs feedback, it needs a copy-editor, a designer for the end product, a marketing and distribution system, maybe even an accountability buddy so that you make your deadline. No matter what you are undertaking, you need to gather an inner-circle team to support the mission and make sure you are left free to concentrate your efforts on the part that turns you on.

This is where the attitude of unapologetic bigness (not arrogance) and self-care immediately kicks in, because whatever role you are casting for your new Evil Empire, always go to the top of the heap and aim for the very best candidate you could possibly wish for, even (and especially) if you think they will be *out of your league.* I want you to drop any idea that just because you are new at this and your project isn't yet flying along and funded that you only deserve team members who are *at your level.* This is a nonsense. There is no one who is out of reach, and if you communicate from your true passion, and this means truly *being* passionate, not *doing* passionate, you will be amazed at the calibre of allies you can manifest.

The first time I was making a film I reached high with amazing results. I didn't consider anyone to be out of reach – they are just people after all – and when you get someone on the phone, whether it is the person you want or their manager or assistant, when you are expressing yourself from your heart with no cringing and fawning, still in your power but not *working it* to impress anyone, it touches the person you are speaking to very deeply. These people are unaccustomed to meeting such raw authenticity, and we all have a natural inclination to participate with and help such people when we come across them. It is so radical to be authentic these days that it has an enigma all of its own, because most people are so comfortable in their hiding, conforming, disempowered state that someone brave enough to simply be real is fascinating. It is very powerful to be visible with your vulnerabilities; it wakes people up. So don't sell yourself short by aiming for people who are halfway down the heap. Go straight to the top. I never imagined I would be able to get the authors Kurt Vonnegut or Tom Robbins in my film, but the connection I made with their 'people' was genuine, and I wasn't attached to them saying yes; I just shared my passion and wish for them to join in with us, and miraculously, though many did say no, there were many who were attracted and said yes.

Being comfortable with the answer 'no' is essential. When you are OK with people saying 'no', you can open yourself up to a whole banquet of 'yes's. Your project deserves the best. You deserve the best. Is there any part of you that resists that idea? Sink into where that feeling and those beliefs live in your body and allow them to dissolve early on, because your ceiling for what you believe you deserve will usually dictate what you receive.

It is very important to make it as easy as possible for people to say yes. When we were trying to get interviews with our heroes or set up recording music sessions with them I would say, 'We'll come to wherever you are, we'll set up our gear, only be with you until you've had enough, and when we've edited you in, we won't ask you to approve it and sign off unless you like it.' You can't make it any more risk-free than that. They don't have to go anywhere, it doesn't have to take a minute longer than they want, and if they don't like what you come up with, it never gets released. It is hard to say no to that even if you are only vaguely interested.

Your passion is a much more enticing commodity than you may imagine. Many of these luminaries who you are going to be approaching were once as driven and turned on as you are, but now, further into their illustrious careers, someone who is as *into it* as you can be like a lifeline to the essence that they have lost touch with. Yes, you will also come up against people who are just too jaded by now to be interested but from a Jedi Knight perspective, those are not the droids you are looking for.

You also have the added advantage that, whereas years ago it was all but impossible to reach your heroes, nowadays with social media and their websites, many of your enquiries go straight to them and you don't even have to deal with the army of managers and agents and appointed protectors. You can go direct to the source. I love this age we are living in for that. Recently I was reading a sci-fi novel by Hannu Rajaniemi, a genius but complex writer who invents all kinds of new words to express his narrative. After I had read three pages in a row and understood nothing I felt frustrated and decided to look for him online. Within a few minutes I had found him on Twitter and wrote him a message asking what certain things meant. Within an hour I received a reply direct from Rajaniemi telling me that it was deliberately written that way but directing me to a website glossary which had some of the translations I needed. Within an hour! And what a cool feeling to be directly in contact with the guy who had written the book I was reading.

When someone gives you a useful contact and you have to reach out to them for the first time, never ever write, telling them all about your project, and then end with 'any help or advice you could give me would be gratefully appreciated'. That is an almost definite way to have your email deleted and never hear from them again. *No one has time to think up what you might need for your project.* It is enough that they have even read your email. If someone leaves it to me to work out what they might need I can't be bothered, but if someone says, 'I am doing a film about shamans and need to find contacts with tribes in South America', I can immediately contact my friend Piers who makes films over there and write a quick email: 'Dear Piers, my friend Jo is looking for contacts with tribes in South America for their shaman film, can you hook them up? Hope you're good, Jamie.' It took me nine seconds, you got something concrete, I am happy with my helpful good deed, and we are all sorted. Be clear what you are asking for and you will often get it. Pick something real that you know they can do and ask for it directly.

In the same vein of making life easy for yourself, always carry with you one of those USB memory sticks. You never know who you are going to find yourself sitting next to on a plane or a train. So often we get chatting to interesting or helpful people as we travel around, and having the ease to be able to keep all your content or images or trailer clips with you at all times and say, 'Hey, look at this,' to someone there and then facilitates all kinds of interesting contacts and hook-ups. As I said, all we can do is make it as likely as possible that our projects will fly. Being able to show people your stuff at any moment is great for optimising the flow of chance meetings.

BE THE BOSS OF YOUR IDEAS

Another area for early dissolving is to get comfortable with everyone being there to serve your idea. Some of us carry fear about looking arrogant, or believe that if we are the leader or boss of a project we might come across as an egomaniac by having the last word on all decisions. It can feel edgy to own the leadership and allow all the geniuses around you to be there for you, to receive what everyone is bringing without shame. These deserving issues can be a huge trap and keep us small. Let others serve you and your idea. It is safe to receive.

If you don't think so, or you have an uncomfortable block arising when you consider this, then it is time to do some dissolving before you take another step. Where did this sheepishness come from? Who planted it in you years ago? Is it someone else's baggage? If so, put it down, because great art, though collaborative, is *not* democratic. No Masterpiece ever came out of a committee, with everyone having their say and arriving at an average, watered-down version of what everyone wants. This endeavour is about *your vision*, it is about a team effort where everyone helps you manifest what is being birthed in you. Yes, we listen to input, and we might even give some of our team decision-making power in areas of the project that we trust them in, but the final word, and there can only be one final word, must come from you. Make sure everyone is on board with this before you set off down the road. A huge part of success is the ability to delegate and harness a team of people's geniuses.

Great art is collaborative but not democratic. It's OK to be the boss.

LET PEOPLE BE GENEROUS TO YOU

Some people feel weird about being given to. The moment someone volunteers 'I'll pay for this one,' they say, 'Oh, no, no . . .' and go into immediate resistance. In this situation I always say to the refuser: 'Safe to receive . . . safe to receive . . .'

It is understandable that those of us who have been given love so transactionally in our lives are cautious to receive it when it's offered, because we have learned since childhood that the payback police are never far behind. When we were little we were taken to the park and bought an ice-cream, and then later maybe taken to a movie, too, but that evening when we didn't obey our parents or carers we were suddenly assaulted with 'I took you to the park. I bought you an ice-cream. I took you to the cinema.' We had no idea during that lovely day that all the while we had been notching up bad credit. No wonder we are suspicious when someone wants to give to us unexpectedly.

But this auto-response hugely limits intimacy and abundance. If you always say no when I try to give you something, then you are never giving me the chance to feel generous and have the lovely experience of giving to you. I want to have my gifts received. We all do. So, be generous in your receiving and generously allow others to feel generous in giving to you.

Every jug needs a cup.

CAN YOU SEND ME SOMETHING?

Now, when you have got Akram Khan to agree to join in with your choreography or Neil Gaiman to cast his eyes over your story outline, the first thing they are going to ask is, 'Can you send me something?' This is where many of us freeze. The document that we need to have ready at this point is crucial to securing their participation. It needs to thrum with your passion as well as communicate clearly what the essence and form of your project is, and it has to do it in a single page. Trust me on this, no matter how great your project is, no one can be bothered to wade through an eight-page version of your big idea, not even that friend of your dad's who said they would help. If anyone sends me something pages long, unless I have already been convinced that I have to be a part of it, I bin it, or if I'm feeling patient I ask them for a one-pager. This is a great discipline, because if you can't get what is great about your project onto a single page I would hazard that there's a major flaw in the idea.

This is the area where any lack of self-belief or belief that you don't deserve success in some way can sabotage the whole thing.

It's time, once and for all, to blow away any cobwebs of past inferiority or unworthiness as we discover what it is exactly we want to express about the essence of our new mission.

Let's play a new game.

Visioning Game

I want you to imagine that you have already finished your project. You have taken what you gathered here, pressed the big red button on your plan, and now it's completed and released to the world.

Your project has been so unbelievably successful that it has gone way beyond anything you could have imagined in your wildest dreams. It has been translated into languages in countries you've never heard of. It has inspired hundreds of spin-off projects in all kinds of fields which have facilitated life-changing shifts in communities all over the world. It has been so far-reaching that all wars have ended, women's rights are fair and upheld globally, it has facilitated a philosophy of abundance and generosity, and boundaries between nations are dissolving. It has inspired the cure for cancer and the end of the arms trade, and the capitalist 'every man for himself' system has melted away and been replaced with a collaborative, mutually respectful and caring culture of plenty. The Dalai Lama has realised there's nothing left to do and is now working at McDonald's (which has gone vegan) in the Happy Meals section, and the friendly aliens have finally deemed our planet fit for first contact. It has been so far-reaching in its impact that *The Sunday Times* (or *Rolling Stone*, or whatever is your preferred rag) are sending over a journalist this week to your home to do an in-depth interview with you for a dedicated twenty-four-page feature about you and your project.

Feel any wriggly resistance?

So the day arrives for the interview, and at some time around mid-morning the bell rings from the lower gate of your estate. You buzz them in knowing it is about a fifteen-minute drive from the entrance to arrive at your front door. You throw something on, and when the doorbell finally goes you decide you will answer it yourself and not send staff, keep it real. You open the front door and there in front of you is an incredibly attractive yet quite bashful and trembly-in-your-presence journalist. You invite them in, make them a cup of chamomile tea, and hold the space for them to calm down a bit before inviting them to take a stroll with you around the grounds to check out the gardens and the new marble around the swimming pool that has just been imported from France.

As you walk and talk you realise how personally touched by your work this journalist is. They really get it. Every question they ask shows you how deeply affected they have been by what you have brought into the world and you answer each of their questions perfectly. You are in an effortlessly articulate flow as you express all your passions and methods and the life lessons that this process brought you. Every word comes out just right, and without even realising the conversation was the interview, you share all that was inspiring and illuminating about your achievements with ease and intimacy.

The next morning the journalist leaves looking a bit ruffled and grateful, and you know in a couple of weeks the magazine will hit the stands and everyone you have ever met will read it. All your ex-lovers, people you went to school with, teachers, relatives, everyone in your life past and present will be reading it. You go down to the village cornershop and pick up your copy. You take it home, open up page one and begin to read . . .

For the next half an hour, write the ultimate, most un-humble fantasy article that could ever be written about you and your project. I want you to totally jump off the deep end into the fantasy of every word you would secretly love to be written about you in your wildest dreams – every word that you would love other people to read about you. This is not an exercise in modesty, quite the opposite. It takes a bit of vulnerability to do this, and you have to park any diligent work you have been doing on your ego for this game. As you write the article, not twenty-four pages, just whatever you can do in the time allotted, you need to be guffawing with your outrageousness, laughing out loud. Leave the ego-aversion stuff in the corner for now. I want you to throw open the floodgates of limitlessness and allow every adjective, every compliment, every accolade to pour forth. You may feel resistance but stay with it, allow this single half-hour period to be totally free of any restraint. Allow yourself to thumb your nose at anyone from your past who might have judgements about you, immersing yourself in total, unadulterated self-aggrandisement and then add something even more outrageous.

Here is a possible structure for the article you might use if you don't want to have to drum it up from nothing.

1) You might start with the journalist's reflections before meeting you, what a huge deal it is for them to have been chosen to be the one who conducts this interview, and why, on a personal level, your work has been so life-changing for them.
2) Then the day of the interview arrives . . . the anticipation.
3) First impressions when you opened the door and they were suddenly in the presence of this wise yet humble maverick.
4) The interview, which usually starts with 'What gave you the idea to do it? What was your inspiration?'

5) Then the actual doing of the project. How did it come together? What was the process of actually bringing it from the Big Idea into manifestation in a form for everyone to be touched by?

6) Once completed, what happened when it was released? How did it spread so far and wide? What actually happened? What did Bono say?

7) And lastly, they usually end on 'And now what's next for you? Where can you go from here?'

8) To conclude the piece I would suggest including some wise parting words from you, something encouraging for the other mere mortals who may want to one day bring their own gifts to the world, and the last thoughts and reflections of the journalist as they take their leave, for ever changed by the experience of meeting you.

You don't have to stick to that structure. I only include it to start you off. Of course, write the piece in any form that feels fun. Write from the point of view of the journalist and do not hold back. Any time you feel resistance, make it even more extravagant. If emotion arises or jarring pangs of inadequacy, take a pause and go inside. Use your Full Body Listening to support you in giving yourself fully to this article and allow even the most Messianic of urges to be satisfied.

The article and vision you now have on the page contains enough content for you to cherry-pick whatever lines and ideas you need and hone the tone for your one-page blast of inspiration.

If you are playing the game in a pair or group you can now go on to the next stage.

We have established what a powerful force our imagination is, yet we are hardly taught in school how best to harness this amazing tool. Once we imagine something we create a reality somewhere where it already exists. The imagination is the channel of creation, and when we combine our imaginations the power of attraction increases exponentially. Having your community or your inner circle supporting and co-visioning your dream delivers astounding results. This is why the Native Americans conduct their vision quest ceremonies. As a group they can generously lend each other the power of their imaginations for the greater good. When we plait together our visioning and imaginative intentions the strength of the lassoo to bring in that reality is massively enhanced, so for this next stage, gather some close friends or members of your project's inner circle and read them your article with total confidence and enjoyment.

While you do this, as the reader, you have to make sure you're not embarrassed or making yourself a joke to deflect the feelings of resistance or shame which may arise. You need to stand tall, unapologetic and fully surrendered to this 'fantasy' reality. This is the key. Those who are listening and supporting you are there to generously lend you their imaginations while you read. So, if there are four of you, the three listeners are all seeing what you are reading in their own imaginations. That is four people's imaginations all visioning the dream together and empowering it with their full belief and approval.

It is important that your listeners are fully present with you throughout the reading, picturing every line as they see it in their mind's eye, because when you have finished, the next stage is that each of your visioning team feed back to you what they saw in their own imaginations while you were reading. You can then weave the best of what you hear into your grand design. Take as long as you like to exchange ideas and inspirations.

Don't limit yourself to the 'reasonable' or 'appropriate' at this stage. Let the vision fly. Allow it to spread its wings with no limits and share your excitement with your group of all the possibilities that could be realised here. If there are four of you in this group, then each of you takes a turn with their own vision and the other three support. I have always enjoyed this way of working and serving each other's visions. When we work in groups of four we end up spending a quarter of the time receiving and three-quarters of the time giving, and this feels like a good formula for generating the best results.

As always, with your Full Body Listening on, you will notice any tightness, any escape urges or resistance to standing proud in your intent. This is both a creative visioning session and a self-cleaning process to blow away the last cobwebs of fake humility that we have been using to not be thought of as too big for our boots and risk rejection. When we play small to play safe we are, in an unvarnished sense, prostituting ourselves to be what we assume other people want. We are editing ourselves down to a less magnificent version of ourselves because we think it will manipulate a better response from whoever we are with. We are suffering for love.

Let's stop treating ourselves this way from now on. Whoever doesn't like us in our full power is not really a friend. Whoever sees me in all my unhinged glory, and stays, they are the people who really love me and *get* me. Those are the people I want to hang out with. I'm done exhausting myself wearing masks for people who I don't want to hang out with anyway. I say take off the masks and see who stays, and remember, worrying and judging yourself for being on an ego-trip *is* an ego-trip.

ACTION STATIONS!

It is time to channel all this wisdom and presence into the action plan for the project. There are numerous models for green-lighting a project, and the one I have found most useful, especially when starting something off unfunded, is a version of a model often used by Disney, DreamWorks and Pixar-type companies. To develop and green-light a new project they split the teams into three camps.

1) The visionaries

These guys are only about the limitless vision. They are not concerned with budgets or schedules, only *what is the most wonderful version of this idea?* They imagine without boundaries and allow themselves full creative licence to bring in the most inspirational and exciting event they can come up with. Then, when they have articulated it clearly, they hand it over to the second group and all go home.

2) The planners

Here, the limitless vision is honed into the most efficient version that is doable with the resources to hand and a thorough to-do list of all and every action needed to bring this idea into form. Then, when they have completed this epic list of actions, duties and, if possible, a level of scheduling and budgeting, they hand it over to the third group and they themselves go home, too.

3) The constructive critics

It is now up to the third group to look at the plan afresh, and rather like an experienced, favourite uncle, they look for problems to fix, areas which need keeping an eye on for problems which may appear later down the line, and ways that the execution of the tasks can be optimised with the current resources. They are like a gardener who has the forward thinking to notice that the tomato plant needs an extra stick of bamboo to support it when the coming weather is unpredictable. They lend their extensive experience to the current plan and constructively wave magic wands of efficiency over the whole blueprint.

For new projects which are not getting going with immediate budgets it is useful to use this template to take the new idea to the stage of being ready for someone else's money, so I recommend getting your three groups together. At first it's OK to have certain inner-circle members occupying more than one group; however, it is essential that when in planning mode, no one is there representing the vision mode. That is, once the vision has been handed over, anyone floating into the next planning group has to consciously put on a different hat and transition from their more feminine, receiving mode into their more masculine, linear mode. Plan a whole day for doing the above three stages, or even dedicate an afternoon to each one so you can be fresh and newly focused for each new flavour of input.

At the end of that process you will have a level one blueprint of the first stage of the project. How it will arrive at the stage for further funding or even directly lifting off will be directed by how the execution of the green-lit plan goes over the next months.

Be sure to apply all the attitudes of self-care and vigilant witnessing on every stage, every meeting, every email, every call. It is how *present* we are when we get busy that will determine the progress and harvest of all the coming work, more than *what* we are doing. Leave space for the unforeseen to exceed your expectations, and never put any disputes or dramas about the project above the humanity and respectful treatment of everyone involved.

> The man who moves a mountain begins by carrying away small stones.
>
> Confucius

This planet requires us to take actions to make our projects fly. Often, the only difference between successful people and those who never got it together is that the successful people carried on taking actions to manifest their dreams and, due to the nature of cause and effect, created a tipping point of accumulated pressure. Persistence and action will eventually create a break. By the laws of probability, after enough concerted action, the sum total of it all and all the creative intentions behind it, will attract what some would call luck but what I see as the natural result of commitment and determination. When we get busy with the inspired but non-attached attitude the forces of support seem to flood towards us.

I believe that all around us, standing to attention, looking sharp in their tailored suits stand God's Deaf Waiters. They are primed and directed to bring us all manner of amazing delights, conjure support we never dreamed of, whisper to us great ideas, and triumphantly manifest unexpected good fortunes to further us on our missions. The only thing is, they are deaf, so they cannot take our orders or understand our desires from what we say we want. They can only understand their orders and our wishes from our actions. When we take actions according to our passions they see us getting busy and productive and they get interested. They conclude, 'Oh, Jamie's doing that, he'll need one of these . . .' and they stylishly come up with timely gifts that we would never have imagined were just what we needed. Summoned by our intent, fuelled by our productivity and commitment, God's Deaf Waiters are all around us, waiting to serve our highest excitements.

Tip big.

BALANCE MASCULINE ACTION WITH FEMININE LISTENING

As you move into the more masculine, action-driven phase of any project, remember to keep turning on your Full Body Listening and checking in with how you feel. If we allow ourselves to be given direction by the more receptive, feminine side then we will keep close to our honesty and authenticity.

Even if you have scheduled to make all your calls on a certain morning, if you make the first one and you get an answer machine, and on the second one they say no, consider stopping making calls that morning and go and do something creative instead. Listen to the flow and don't push the river. Sometimes you can have a really fixed idea about how the day should go, or how a part of the project should run, but everything seems to be conspiring to scupper your plans. How would it be if we decided to trust that maybe Life had an improved plan for us?

MEETINGS

There is probably going to come a time in the life of your project where you will need to meet with people who might give you financial backing or invest in your project by sharing their resources or contacts with you. It is vital that you don't take these meetings too seriously and get yourself in a pickle, thinking there is something make-or-break about this meeting. There isn't. We have no idea or control of how the resources we need will come, and if this meeting isn't a fit, another one will be. If you still find yourself feeling nervous while you are waiting to be seen, just smile to yourself and return to the breath. Even give yourself a little chuckle before you go in and return to the lightness and trust, in full acknowledgement that there is zero control and we are all just showing up, doing our best and trusting whatever the chaos brings.

For me, rule number one is: *never pretend you like someone more than you really do to get their money*. Yes, I know this is totally contrary to most business practices, which teach the best ways to *get something out of this person*, and the misuse of techniques such as NLP offers a menu of manipulations to get what you want, but for me I would run a mile from such practices. My rule of thumb is that if I wouldn't feel comfortable having this person in my treehouse, I don't take their money. It is dishonest to take someone's investment under false pretences of liking them. If they knew what you really thought of them they wouldn't give you the money, so I urge you to be sincere and never take any money from a source which causes you to bury how you really feel. It never comes to any good.

Another thing to look out for are *abundance portals*. These are golden moments of possibility where you step through unexpected doorways which open up suddenly. Always be watchful for them. For instance, there is a golden time towards the end of each meeting where everyone thinks the meeting is over and that what they came to talk about has been covered, but you haven't put on your coat yet. This has proved to be one of the most high-yield abundance portals of my career. Everyone relaxes, and during the niceties as you wrap it up you may find yourself talking about something which has nothing to do with this meeting and suddenly the penny drops that *this* is the reason you came here today.

I have never once got the budget I was looking for from the meeting I was supposed to. Not once!

Years ago, after the success of the first 1 Giant Leap film and album, I met Annie Lennox at a party in Mallorca and she invited me to get busy devising her videos for her new album. I was over the moon. We hung out in London as she recorded her *Bare* album and we chatted about creative possibilities. I was really into it and even did storyboards for my ideas, which I have never done in my life before or since. As the album came to its completion, the day came for me to meet her manager, a guy called Simon Fuller whom I was unfamiliar with (typical – he was only the most successful entertainment entrepreneur in the country, having co-created the Spice Girls and *Pop Idol*), and I went off to his Battersea office to show him my stuff.

I found it a bit weird entering that building. As I was shown to his office I was definitely being peered at from behind desks. I later found out that Simon rarely conducts external meetings and no one knew who this scruffy hippy was who was defiling their newly polished leather sofas. He greeted me warmly but within ten minutes he shared with me that Annie's record label in America were so cross about her choice of cover artwork that they'd pulled the video budgets and sadly we weren't going to be making them this time.

I was disappointed, but my head didn't drop. It didn't look like the meeting was going to go on much longer, but before I had my coat on he asked me in passing, 'So what are you going to do with the next Giant Leap?' I was shocked that he had even heard of it. I had him pegged as Mr Mainstream and certainly not a customer for our world music meets spiritual philosophy epic. *Oh Jamie, when will you learn to stop pigeon-holing people?* I told him plainly that we never wanted another record deal as long as we lived, that we felt they were like a bank with the worst interest rate in the world, and what we really wanted was a partner in some sort of 50:50 split with our creativity and their money. That felt fair to me. I wasn't in pitching mode, as I didn't think for a minute our marginalised art could ever be of interest to this super-mainstream corporation. Yet as I spoke, his eyes went to a faraway place and he started slowly nodding. He interrupted me: 'Yes, yes, I agree with that. You see that guy over there?' He pointed through the glass wall of his office to a dude in a tie and shirt sleeves who looked busy. 'That's my head of accounts. Show him your numbers . . .' I had unwittingly stumbled into an abundance portal and within a week they'd approved $3 million for us to make *1 Giant Leap 2: What About Me?*

I feel certain that a huge part of what inspired him to back us was the 'we're doing it anyway' attitude. Never project the idea that you need their money to do what you want to do. They are one of many sources where the funds could come from. There is no pressure or need for them to fund you, as you are doing it with or without their money. It is fascinating to see children playing when they don't know they're being watched. They are doing what they are doing for them, not you, and that's very attractive. When we see a band on stage, it is the ones who are playing for their own kicks which turn us on, so much more than entertainers who are there to please you.

Can you be totally yourself in the meeting even when there is a huge amount of money at stake? It is a great opportunity to observe yourself and how you might be attracted to change your authentic version of yourself to fit with your idea of what they need to see.

The Taoist poet Chuang Tzu expresses this through the art of archery:

> When an archer is shooting for nothing he has all his skill.
> If he shoots for a brass buckle he is already nervous.
> If he shoots for a prize of gold
> he goes blind
> or sees two targets
> – he is out of his mind!
> His skill has not changed. But the prize
> divides him. He cares.
> He thinks more of winning than of shooting
> and the need to win
> drains him of power.

It is a powerful practice to notice how your desire makes you less authentic, more watchful and therefore less natural. We get our best results when we are so relaxed that our natural flow articulates everything perfectly with no effort. The moment we 'mind' what happens, our desire can disconnect us from our innate genius as the more masculine part of us attempts to control the situation. As usual, the very thing that 'control' does to manipulate the situation is the thing that becomes self-defeating. Use the things you mind about to notice this happening and then soften back into the trusting, feminine witness again.

MONEY

would like to dispel, once and for all, the idea that if you had an extra ten million in the bank that it would in some way be a bad thing, that it would make you shallow or selfish, or relegate you to the club of the greedy rich. The truth is that if you had an extra ten million in the bank you would do wonderful generous things with it. You would fund all kinds of projects and initiatives that were good for the planet. You would support people you know in fulfilling their dreams. I know some of you might blanch at that idea and feel ashamed at the thought of being stinking rich, but just consider it for a moment. If you had all that money wouldn't you spend it on progressive, good-for-everyone stuff? Of course you would (after you got back from your world tour and gold-plated your laptop). So let's lose this whole 'I'm holy when I'm skint' attitude. It is part of the old suffering paradigm that got us into this mess in the first place. I dare you to include yourself in the idea of wealth.

So, when you are paying yourself from whatever budget you have raised, pay yourself the absolute maximum the budget will allow without being absurd and leaving the project short of what it needs. You being paid really well doesn't mean you're greedy.

There are three things I'd like you to buy yourself when you've finished this chapter.

1) Do me a favour and buy yourself a nice bag with *a good zip*. Stop buying the crappiest version of everything as of *now*. You deserve a nice bag with a good zip, and, trust me, you won't be lying there on your deathbed regretting spending the extra £30 or £40. You will be pleased you treated yourself as you deserve to be treated.

2) Get yourself a really nice towel. You know when you stay somewhere posh and you get out of the shower and the touch of that expensive towel is borderline orgasmic? You have to share it with everyone downstairs at dinner. 'Have you had a shower? Did you check out the towels here?' Everyone deserves a good towel. Get rid of that nasty synthetic one you have which just rearranges the moisture around your body without actually drying you. We wash too often to scrimp on having at least one wonderful towel in our lives.

3) Make sure you own at least one pair of either really good-quality speakers or headphones. Music is too important to not have at least one place in your life where you can immerse yourself in great sound quality. I would like to start a charity that made sure everyone on the planet had access to clean water and wonderful-quality musical sound.

You don't have to break the bank at Monte Carlo to achieve these three things but they have far-reaching implications on what we feel we deserve.

How we spend the money we have is hugely indicative of our beliefs around abundance and well worth paying attention to. Money may not be able to buy you happiness but it has huge potential energy, and when we spend it, by the law of cause and effect, we send out a quality of thought into the world with each payment. I remember getting locked out of my flat in the middle of the night and having to call a locksmith to get back in. The guy came and it cost about £180, which was an annoying blow to the coffers. Usually I would be on a downer as I handed it over but this time I remembered how powerful the way in which we hand over money can be, and as I got out the cash I imagined the locksmith's wife going around the supermarket and buying an organic chicken this week and a video game for young Ian who did so well in his maths test . . . I got a bit carried away, but you get the picture. Sometimes you are going to be spending thousands and thousands at once. It is important to do it with positivity and grace, and even if you don't fully believe me do it anyway, just in case I'm right. Even if it is a parking ticket and you feel resentful, in fact especially then, you can either look at the parking fine as a drag or you can look at it as a reminder that you are wealthy enough to pay this lump and it doesn't collapse your life. As usual, it is all in how we choose to frame it.

FEEDBACK FOR YOUR GENIUS

I have always been a 'Mummy, don't look at my picture until it's finished' kind of a child, and it is always vulnerable to let people see or hear unfinished work. Whenever a musician plays you their demo you can rarely listen to it, because all the way through they are saying things like 'we haven't balanced the bass on this yet' or 'the drums haven't been mixed properly yet', so anxious are they about sharing work in progress that is by its very definition imperfect.

We need to get past that anxiety in the later stages of a project because feedback just before the end can be crucial. Choose five or six people who aren't part of the project to see it with fresh eyes just before the end and listen to their feedback. Don't worry too much about negative feedback that only one person offers. No one individual's opinion or taste is more important than yours, but if three or more all point to the same area where they got lost or lost interest, then it is definitely worth addressing. You might think you have nailed it and been totally clear, but if three of the feedback team all point out the same thing, the chances are many others will too. Consider it as a great blessing to have the chance to improve it. I don't believe you should compromise your artistic integrity based on feedback or ever change an element of the project in a way that isn't to your taste just because 'it didn't test well in Cleveland', but within the boundaries of what you feel is in harmony with the project, your audience (not necessarily everyone) getting it is important.

If you have been working with others on their projects throughout this process, then the next exercise may seem a little unexpected. I was once working with an artist who was at the stage of their career where they couldn't have been flying any higher. Millions and millions of albums sold, headlining every festival for insane amounts of cash, on the cover of every named magazine, awards and countless avid fans in every country of the world that allowed pop music to be played there. It is so ironic that even with all that success, it was that one tiny, bitchy review on the *Portsmouth Herald* website or some other utterly insignificant portal that punctured the balloon of fun and went in deeper than you would think proportionate. This is a lesson worth heeding. Somehow we tend to get much more affected by the negative things that are written or said about us than the glorious things. These criticisms, especially when mean, can cut you right to the candlewick. This is why we never leave the project birthing process without playing the following game, which is a kindness, an immunisation if you will, so that nothing anyone could ever say or write about you or your project in the future will be able to hurt you.

So, swap notebooks with the someone you have been co-supporting projects with, and take just ten minutes to write for them the worst, gossipy, mean-spirited, missing-the-point review of their idea that could ever be written. Yes, yes, I know it seems harsh, but this is a loving thing to do and is a hilarious opportunity to allow your shadow off the leash in a safe way and fully enjoy yourself in the process! You are immunising them. You are going to write something so loathsome and malicious that there is nothing anyone could ever write or say in the future about their mission that could top it. Any bad review they ever get in the future couldn't hold a candle to your malevolent 200-word review. Just let it all hang out, unless the person you are writing it for asks you to pull your punches. Go dark, and don't forget that the final sentence has to be the death blow. The last words have to kill it beyond any hope of resuscitation.

When you have finished it, enjoy reading the reviews to each other with unapologetic relish. In the workshops, somehow, it delivers more tears of laughter and beautiful intimacy than any of the other games.

CHAPTER 11

Call to Action

It's 3:23 in the morning
and I'm awake
because my great great grandchildren
won't let me sleep
my great great grandchildren
ask me in dreams
what did you do while the planet was plundered?
what did you do when the earth was unraveling?

surely you did something
when the seasons started failing

as the mammals, reptiles, birds were all dying?

did you fill the streets with protest
when democracy was stolen?

what did you do
once
you
knew?

'heiroglyphic stairway', Drew Dellinger

I thought about calling this book *Stating the Obvious*, because all I am doing is trying to help people be aware of the gifts they already have, gifts that have been there all along, hanging out in the shadows. Really what I am about is helping people to let go of all the 'limitations', to show you my own wounds and insanity and voices so that you might feel more comfortable about coming into the room with your own. Yes, I am often a mess, and that's OK with me. It is our unvarnished selves that hold our true capacity for intimacy, creativity and connection, not the clipped and edited versions of ourselves we present to the world, all the while fearful that our demons will jump out (as they always do) uninvited at the most embarrassing, crippling times.

I've said many times that in my workshops and in all my dealings in life my own mission is to create an army of 'walking permission slips', a legion of like-minded souls who, just by being ourselves – present, authentic, often vulnerable – become catalysts for everyone who comes into contact with us to evolve playfully and be exactly as they are without the need to exhaust themselves wearing masks. When we meet people like this, who are comfortable to be seen and heard just as they are, without hiding behind roles or being an 'appropriate' version of themselves, we ourselves become more relaxed and more authentic. Our freedom to be seen in our mess, in our eccentricity, in our fallibility, creates a permission in everyone we meet to lighten up around all the sides of themselves they believe aren't welcome.

Let's create a revolution of visibility, authenticity and playfulness. It's available. When we speak freely about the parts of ourselves that usually get skipped or hidden, we become walking permission slips for everyone else to come out of their painful, lonely hiding and join in. The stigma and this unhealthy, un-self-loving practice of hiding and faking begins to dissolve, but only by example.

One key purpose of the Facebook groups I've set up ('Bad Parents of The World, Unite!', 'Sanctuary for Terror', 'Being with My Rage', 'The Treasure Hunt of Mental Illness') is to destigmatise the shame of the raw, edgy, culturally-pushed-away sides of our lives and experiences. The 'shame' or 'resistance' people feel to share their most vulnerable experiences is one of the great diseases of our culture. We have all supported the wrong idea that it is not OK to be simply yourself, having the challenging experiences you are having and be seen in them. This hiding, this 'I couldn't let anyone know the truth' belief, is a core reason our culture is so screwed up, fake and shame-ridden. It is the opposite of the intimate life we all really want.

I want to promote a culture where we become a bit more interested in feeling and become more fascinated with the feelings that go off in our chest and solar plexus when someone pisses us off, or when a project or person excites us. We are so in rejection of our explosive volcanic feelings that go off when someone upsets us, we will do anything not to feel it. We will fight, condemn, manipulate – all external things that stop us from feeling. Equally, we have been taught to push down feelings of bigness, so that our Masterpieces are left to languish out beyond the reaches of our comfort zones. If we decide instead to become fascinated with what's going on inside us, to tune in to the listening field, that is the ticket to freedom.

THE TWIN TRAIL

Planet Earth is a theme park of incalculably diverse, possible experiences. We have everything here: from the angelic, generous, heart-bursting and ecstatic to the cruel, violent, destructive and toxic. This planet offers an endless spectrum of limitations and illuminations. We have noble expressions of heart-breaking courage side by side with destructive corruption and harrowing acts of ignorance. We have disease and abuse and gun-runners and addiction and despair, there are disappearing species, environmental destruction, shame and disconnection from each other, over-reactive relationship breakdowns and a terror of loneliness all over the place, while there are illnesses and betrayals, and even the inevitable approach of a final human death itself. You could also look at Earthworld as the ultimate theme park of limitation. It is as if any challenging scenario you could possibly think of to experiment with is on offer here.

However, for this game to work, you have to take a forgetting pill on the way in. The admission fee is that you have to forget any Oneness place you came from and really believe you are an individual. You have to think that when this human body you've been given to have your adventure in hits seventy or eighty years, you'll die, and that'll be it. You have to fully believe you are an individual for this theme park of experience to work, and although you get to have an incredible spectrum of light and dark experiences, what also comes with being an individual is loneliness, competitiveness, isolation and self-doubt. It is a high price to pay for the ticket, and navigating the sudden aloneness can be confusing and hazardous if no one taught you what the game was.

Many people believe that there's some sort of a unifying Oneness that connects us all, a non-dualistic All That Is thing that we all 'come from' – and within the wonderful diversity of cultures and individuals on this planet that One Source is expressed and sought out in thousands of different, beautiful, lyrical ways. Whether through divine entities like God, or the idea of a higher self that lives within each of us, in nature and art and sexuality or even connecting to the great fluffy dolphin in the sky, in the realm where this Oneness exists, the great limitation is that here there can be no diversity of experience, just the ommming Oneness vibrating in undivided bliss.

This Oneness realm is great, don't get me wrong, but to have a diversity of experience we need to move to the realm of duality, the realm of solid matter, where there's 'me' and 'everything else' to touch and taste and see and hear and feel. To immerse myself in the epic menu of experiences that are available here in this Earthworld theme park we're born into, there has to be not Oneness but Twoness. For all experiences there needs to be Me (the experiencer) and pizza (the thing I'm experiencing). There needs to be Me and music, or Me and You. There needs to be duality. So, we incarnate into this material earth plane as individuals, apparently separate from each other and everything else around us, to expose ourselves to an almost infinite menu of possible encounters, some pleasurable and some painful.

If we do decide to be activists in our work, in our relationships and with ourselves, then the journey we need to take is a Twin Trail. We travel alone and at the same time together, so that whatever mission or cause we choose is framed as both a journey *out* into the world to make a difference and a journey deep *into* our own selves to receive and work through the many illuminations and challenges that this cause represents for us personally.

Whatever area you have been inspired to involve yourself in says something about you. You don't just choose your cause randomly. Your choice reflects something uniquely relevant to you and your own personal journey. This requires some sober reflection. For example, there is a personal reason the folk who are protesting in the Occupy movement, especially in areas such as Wall Street, choose corruption and greed as their nemesis. We may ask ourselves:

How do these issues reflect on me?

Why am I stimulated and triggered by this particular cause?

How is Life's genius trying to show me myself and invite me back to authenticity and wholeness?

Unless these questions are being asked daily I never fully trust another activist or myself.

LIVING ON HEART MOUNTAIN

For me, I am a provoker and a disruptor, a wind-up merchant and a tail puller, a prodder and a poker. When I meet someone's 'appropriate' mask my first impulse is to want to dance with them to the edge of their 'appropriate' version of themselves and see what illuminating fun can be had when the mask slips. Suddenly, then, there's a chance of intimacy and often some well-needed oxygen.

When I was a child I soon learned, as did the other children, that when I got things right and obeyed my carers I was awarded the kisses, prizes and approval. Most kids worked it out pretty quickly. Get it right and the computer goes <ping!>. Pass the test <ping!>. Tie the shoelace <ping!>. Sit down nicely <ping!>. Add up the numbers <ping!>. Be a good boy <ping!> <ping!> <ping!>. But the problem with being intelligent and curious is that before very long the <ping!> noise becomes predictable and boring – even claustrophobic at times.

And then one soon discovers that when you get it 'wrong' the computer does something much more interesting. It goes <dn%fkj*erbfk!> or <nd$eg£rfnjh!> and always in a uniquely insightful way! As the wonderful word artist Jenny Holzer once wrote: 'Spit a mouthful of milk over someone if you want to learn something about their personality fast.'

So, my natural fascination led me to become labelled a 'problem child' – always in trouble and always puzzled by the injustice of it. Since that time I have never lost my excitement to explore the edges where 'normal', repetitive, robotic and safe codes of behaviour can be disrupted and dissolve into laughter, creativity, foolishness and numerous epiphanies. I want to question and challenge the dishonest, violently self-edited 'brochure' of ourselves that we each present to the world. We have become so used to being fake and hiding who we really are inside. I no longer wish to feed that sleepy, unconscious agreement we seem to have all made not to trigger each other, not challenge each other and not say what we see or how we really feel.

But there is one rule that, even amongst the culture of being a rule-free shaker-upper of things, must be observed, and that is that no matter whose tail I am pulling, whose ego I am challenging, whose mask I am slipping, if I am *in any way* coming from even a shred of superiority, elitism, point-scoring or self-aggrandisement then my offering is toxic as hell.

I have learned in this opening up to honesty that I need to be fully open-hearted at all times – what I now call Heart Mountain, and then with any gift I give, any twopenny's worth I throw into the soup, I can be fully responsible and loving and hold the space with confidence and fascination for whatever might arise. If I am trying to prove something to the person I am challenging, if I am feeding back to them without full empathy and knowledge of my own fallibility and foolishness, then I am likely going to start a fight, shut someone down, or even, as has happened to me upon occasion, be physically assaulted.

Heart Mountain is the key to all communication, especially the tender stuff. Heart Mountain is connected to the earth. Heart Mountain is still and always listening and observing without judgement. It is located in the listening, feminine field. When I know I am centred in Heart Mountain I can dare to express my edgiest, most risky offerings with confidence. From Heart Mountain I can be steadfast in the face of all criticism and complaint and never need to defend or argue.

CHANGING THE WORLD

I would also like to offer the idea that maybe the world doesn't *need* changing, but that doesn't mean we shouldn't try to make a difference. I realise this is not the easiest of cases to make; after all what is the point of doing all this deep journeying if we aren't then going to change the world for the 'better' in some way, but stick with me here. Because from one perspective you could look at planet earth as the planet of limitation, a place for souls to come and experiment with every combination of dark and light that you could ever imagine. We have diseases and addictions and violence and corruption here. We have polluted soil, polluted water and polluted air. We have almost no laws or limitations on the ongoing destruction of the world's eco-system, even though we know quite well this is the only habitable planet we could ever live on. We are seeing species of animals disappearing every day, gone for ever. We have countless fatal and debilitating diseases, and a medical and pharmaceutical system that cares only about the money it can make from illnesses, not the preventative or healing processes for them. We have an education system that barely gives a nod to the wealth of imagination and unique gifts of our children but channels them all through an archaic, purely academically designed conveyer belt to produce good, obedient worker bees with low expectations and weeds out the free-thinkers, rebels and mavericks at a very early stage. We have a military system, which rather than focus on protecting the people from the unspeakable horrors of war, actively makes and sells guns and bombs to as many countries as possible to increase the amount of death and destruction on the planet and profit economically from the carnage. This is the planet of limitation, and perhaps we all come here to earth world for that very reason. Maybe it is *meant* to be fucking scary.

It seems like at every period in history the people of earth have been fearing Armageddon, replaying over and over the terror fed to them in the apocalyptic holy books. Look at the last century. In the 1940s it was the Second World War, then for twenty years after that it was the communists and the ever-present threat of nuclear war. Then came drug addictions and AIDS followed by ecological disaster, global warming, the re-enslavement of black America through their money-making prison system in which white-owned prisons sell forced black labour for profit to high-street companies. Then terrorism and the faked war on terrorism to justify more and more profiteering from the guns and bombs we make, and the controlling and stealing of various countries' oil and other national resources while scaring the shit out of everybody. We have always had *something* to be terrified about, and it could be possible that all the 'changing the world' we want to do is no more effective than dismantling the mechanical shark at the *Jaws* exhibit at Universal Studios.

Maybe it is all there to awaken our compassion, our outrage and our will to create something better, but as an ongoing process with no finish line. This wouldn't mean that it isn't worth getting stuck in, but always, as with our creative projects, following our inspiration *with no attachment to outcome.*

LET'S BE HONEST

It is easier for us all to live in a culture of blame while we turn a blind eye to actions that are taken so that we can all stay in our comfort zones of smartphones, exotic foods and cheap consumer products. It is easier to pretend to ourselves that we are powerless while all the time we make choices that reinforce the violence and corruption. It is easier to be angry at governments for doing nothing to take better care of our planet, and yet we continue to vote for them, drive our cars, fly abroad and throw half our food away. It is easier to pretend that we are small rather than stand up in all our bigness and shout from the mountain top.

We love this comfort zone so much that we are OK with our leaders killing people far away, keeping poor people 'over there' enslaved, and destroying environments and species across the water and even at home so that we can exist in our lovely coddled bubble. We can't pretend we don't know, and we sometimes care a bit, maybe enough to click a petition on Facebook – but even the so-called awake ones, even those of us who know quite a lot about what's going on, do comparatively little about it.

Years ago, when we transitioned from the George Bush regime to the Obama government, it seemed like there was going to be a massive shift in how the whole system of resources and the military would be governed. There was so much excitement about Obama getting in that many activists went to sleep. It seemed as if the battle had been won and we could all relax. The truth is that very little changed, and worse, a huge percentage of juicy activism vanished overnight, imagining that this lovely Obama dude would now sort everything out. This could have been the most genius act of controlled opposition ever. At least when the Bush governments were in charge everyone was motivated to stand up for their beliefs and gather together to make the changes our planet so badly needed. There was a wonderful community of activists linking up all over the world, on the streets, on the internet – a really cohesive movement coming together. Then, when Obama got in, everyone thought, *We've done it! Yes, we can!* And believed the battle had been won. This was the worst day for activism on the planet. Let's wait for the actual results of our new leaders, even if we're sure we trust them, before we shut up shop and pack up the placards.

As I allow myself to be more honest and visible in my work and my relationships, I know that I want more from myself, my choices and my actions. Anita Roddick told me that the only way to turn this around is through the 'vigilante consumer', that unless we choose more carefully what we spend our money on, nearly every penny we spend is unconsciously funding the brutality. We need to know, when we buy at a certain store or fill up our cars at a certain petrol station, who we are funding, because if we all decided to be totally clean about where we spend our money every day, the companies and structures that perpetrate this destruction would have no more funds to carry on.

> If you think you are too small to make a difference, try sleeping with a mosquito.
>
> Dalai Lama

Noam Chomsky told me that we are all educated to believe that 'there's nothing we can do', that our 'free' culture's media is directed to brainwash us into feeling powerless, but the truth is, in a culture like ours, 'you can do a lot'. He calls it 'the engineering of consent' and says that all through school we are directed to believe that success means becoming a millionaire, but there are other values. These are the values you have been discovering as you begin to fully feel and question your addiction to approval, when you begin to ask not 'what *should* I do?' but 'what excites and *attracts* me?'.

So . . . shall we? Can we make a start by foregoing some creature comforts so that less power and money streams into the hands of the corporate oligarchs? What would you be prepared to give up? I'm writing this on an Apple computer, probably made in a Chinese sweatshop where someone jumped out of the window to their death due to horrific working conditions.

The crazy thing is that sustainable change could happen tomorrow if we collectively decided as one force to go for it. I get so excited for that moment. Now that we have the internet we can instantly communicate and gather as one. Is that day coming?

I've stopped eating meat because the factory farming industry is inhumane and backward.

I haven't stopped using petrol in my car.

I have started buying my vegetables locally and am learning how to grow my own, but I still buy some products from the big chains who sell aisles and aisles of toxic, processed food and care nothing for your or your family's health.

I also want to flag the necessity of dissolving all need for revenge and public shaming. We don't need our enemies to crumble in flames of justice, we just need to build a new system that makes those sociopaths redundant. Any part of us that wants the kind of justice where we all get to be 'right' and 'superior' is asking for trouble. Let's build the new, not complain about the old. Let's not use these clowns to play out our repressed vengeance issues – even if we do feel totally justified. It is a sucker punch to be righteous and often falsely justifies the perpetuation of violence.

'Vengeance is mine sayeth the Lord' is actually a very compassionate line. When we personally get involved punishing or meting out what we perceive as deserved retribution to individuals or groups of people, even in small ways – when we take it upon ourselves to be the judge and executor of our notion of 'justice', even if the receiver is undeniably 'wrong' – we make trouble for ourselves by involving ourselves in that person's story.

Beware choosing to be the punisher or the righteous deliverer of justice. It's hazardous to humans, not gods.

Who are the most unforgivable people on earth? We all seem to have culturally agreed that sex offenders, rapists and especially child abusers are totally unforgivable and deserving of zero compassion, just condemnation. I feel we are all trapped as a culture while we keep those groups locked in the eternal dungeon, so I want to, inch by inch, gently consider how those abusers became like that. I know it stirs people up, and had anything ever happened to one of my own kids I would probably find it impossible to react in any other way, but I'm exploring this for a sincere reason. As long as we are unable to open up this unforgivable, taboo conversation we will remain trapped in the Dark Ages.

I believe that people who have been abused will fall into two camps: those who afterwards were lucky enough to be exposed to ideas, people, luck/destiny that gave them the chance to make healthier, non-abusive choices; and those who just got more violence and rape and abuse and punishment and shame and alienation, and who became too damaged in the complexity of their experiences to make a healthy choice and often became abusers. I believe those people who are mentally ill need high-security hospitals, not self-righteous and over-simplistic condemnation.

Take the baby day by day until it becomes the abuser, orchestrating the abuse. Slowly watch his or her life day by day – all the complex things that happened to it. Four years old abused . . . Six years old abused . . . Nine years old now twisted and lost . . . Thirteen years old with no exposure to anything but hatred and ignorance . . . Sixteen years old getting into real violence . . . Until they become a full-on abuser, and choose which day you cut off your compassion. If you want to be free, try this exercise.

Sometimes people say, 'But what if this happened to one of your kids?' My answer is if that happened I would undoubtedly be too traumatised at first to speak or act from anything other than my trauma, I would not be of sound mind, and my judgements and actions would be destructive. But just because I would find it almost impossible to practise what I've written above in that situation does not make the position less valid. I hope I would eventually encounter someone who would help me somehow seek out compassion and understanding. Ironically, those who have sought out compassion and understanding for their abusers have found it the healthiest and quickest route to transforming both their own trauma and that of the abuser. Condemning and shaming has never helped a single victim or abuser; if anything, it has entrenched their trauma deeper. It is the victim's innocence that needs to be upheld and affirmed.

I support and welcome and am grateful to all those who join me on this visible journey, bravely being the first to be seen in all their mess, so that others can have more comfort with theirs. In the 1970s it was a taboo to get divorced, and sharing experiences of unhappy marriages was also taboo – it would only have happened in closed groups. These days it's no longer taboo, and people are getting the support they need, but it took brave people earlier on (including my mum) to be seen, who gave everyone else the comfort. Let's be braver and participate in the destig-matising of our basic truths and needs.

Please be a walking permission slip with me – lots of people need the example of your permission to dare to be free themselves and receive the support they need.

I'm copying my manifesto here again. Why not put down this book and go and write your own?

THE MANIFESTO

- We want to put our own full, unedited, unabbreviated selves into the work.
- We want to create a movement of introspection and self-enquiry where the viewer becomes the subject of the piece. It's about you.
- We want to dare to show ourselves in all our raw glory, really express what's going on in the chaos and the shadows, then give ourselves the chance to connect to something real in our audience. Because when I talk about me, you'll hear about you.
- We need collectively to admit that we're not fine, we're not confident and balanced and good.
- We turn up to work every day pretending we're not neurotic and obsessed and insatiable and full of doubt, and we waste so much energy keeping up this mutual pretence for each other because we think if people saw the truth, if people really knew what was going on in our heads, all the crazy truth of our dark appetites and self-loathing, then we'd be rejected. But in fact, the opposite is true. It is when we dare to reveal the truth that we unwittingly give everyone else permission to do the same.
- We need to stop holding our breath for a moment and actually come into the room. Be here, present, vulnerable and authentic.
- If we can all collectively acknowledge our insanity, the amount of energy we'll inherit that has been wasted on the mask will be enough to creatively solve any global crisis. We are on a mission to make self-reflection hip for just a moment, just long enough to save us.

Acknowledgements

Thank you to Raisa, my Love and partner in crime, my daughters India Rose, Lola Mae and Memphis. Thank you to their Mothers and my Mother and all the Mothers. Thank you to the Fathers who are dissolving centuries of ignorance from their ancestry and evolving a new generation of Men leading through Love and Service. Thank you to all the wonderful teachers of the NOW lineage from Ram Dass to Eckhart Tolle. Thank you to Bruce Frantzis for his generous Chi. Thank you to Bashar for the clearest transmissions. Thank you to Duncan for all your incredible creative genius and all the extra miles. Thank you to Malissa and Ewan and Milarepa for helping me keep this show on the road. Thank you to everyone I've forgotten to thank. Thanks to Kate and Canongate and to Miranda for making me eat food while I wrote this.